A MARVELOUS GUIDE TO THE WIZARDING WORLD OF HARRY POTTER

1st Edition

TABLE OF CONTENTS

INTRODUCTION

Hello! Thank you for choosing to browse this book! You must be currently visiting, planning a future vacation, or excited to learn more about Universal Studios Hollywood! No matter your reason, we are ecstatic that you trust us to be your information center for all things Universal Studios Hollywood!

WHAT YOU WILL LEARN

This book was written with *you* in mind to learn all about Universal Studios Hollywood located in California! Our team of travel advisors and planners decided we wanted to share with you all the useful information we have gained over years of planning Universal Studios Hollywood vacations.

Here is some of the exciting and useful information you will find in this book:

- Best Times to Visit
- Studio Tour Information
- Recommendations of Local, Nearby Hotels
- Details on the Upper and Lower Lot and CityWalk
- Annual Seasonal Events
- Things to Do in the Surrounding Area including Dining Recommendations
- Insider Tips and Tricks
- Fun and Interesting Facts
- Accessibility Information
- .... AND MORE!

WHO ARE WE?

We would like to give you a little history about us! Marvelous Mouse Travels (MMT) is a team of travel advisors and planners who all share a common love of travel and adventure. Marvelous Mouse Travels began in the summer of 2014 when owner, Kari Dillon, branched out on her own after years of assisting clients with various travel requests. Now, with about 300 agents across the United States, the Marvelous Mouse Travels' team assists clients around the world with all of their domestic and international travel needs.

Why use our services for your next Universal Studios Hollywood vacation? Marvelous Mouse Travels is the first Universal Diamond

Agency in the nation and was named the 2019 Top Travel Agency for Universal Resorts. All MMT agents are certified Universal Specialists, meaning we have been extensively trained in everything Universal can provide our clients. Many agents also have first hand experience visiting Universal Studios Hollywood and its surrounding areas, allowing us to better assist you with recommendations and information. This book focuses solely on Universal Studios Hollywood located in California, but we have also written two other guide books about Universal Orlando Resort: "A Marvelous Guide to Universal Orlando Resort" (e-book) and "A Marvelous Guide to the Wizarding World of Harry Potter" (available in e-book and paperback) on Amazon.

WHAT WE DO

We provide top-notch planning services at NO CHARGE to you! We are paid directly by the vendors, not by the clients! When you book a trip with Marvelous Mouse Travels, we are dedicated to helping you plan a vacation full of memories that will last a lifetime! We, collectively, have extensive knowledge of Universal Studios Hollywood, and we will put that knowledge to work for you. With any budget, we can customize an adventurous or leisure getaway that will meet your family's needs! We will work together with you throughout the entire process to make sure the best vacation is planned at the best value. We do the work; you have the fun! Some of our services include:

- Quoting vacation packages, ticket only purchases, and more
- Booking vacation packages, ticket only purchases, and more
- Assisting with any additional needs such as ADA accommodations and service animals
- Setting up dining reservations (as able)
- Applying additional promotions to reservations to ensure clients are receiving the best price available
- Making payments on vacation packages
- Notating special requests and celebrations
- Assisting with tickets and/or accommodations to other local destinations such as Disneyland
- Planning daily itineraries
- Providing numerous tips and tricks before your vacation
- Reserving airport transfers or assisting with local transportation (as able)

COMMON TERMS AND PHRASES

Throughout this book, you will see commonly used Universal Studios Hollywood phrases and abbreviations. They have been listed below for your convenience.

MMT- Marvelous Mouse Travels agency

Fun Fact- Fun facts about different areas of the destination

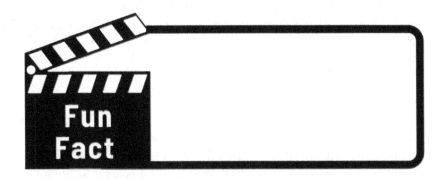

Pro Tip- Quick insider tips compiled by Marvelous Mouse Travels' agents to create the best vacation experience for you

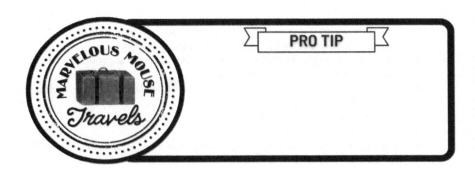

MMT Favorite- Marvelous Mouse Travels' agents' favorite restaurants/food, rides, special events, and more

SNW- Super Nintendo World

WWOHP- Wizarding World of Harry Potter

Now that you know more about Universal Studios Hollywood and Marvelous Mouse Travels, continue reading and let the adventure begin!

For more information or a no obligation vacation quote, contact Marvelous Mouse Travels at www.marvelousmousetravels.com/contactus **or one of the agents directly through their contact information in the next section!**

MEET THE AUTHORS
Kari Dillon
(info@marvelousmousetravels
.com)

Favorite Ride: Mario Kart:
Bowser's Challenge

Kari is the owner of
Marvelous Mouse Travels.
Her love for Universal has
allowed her to develop an
excellent partnership with

Universal. Through this partnership, the agency has multiple
opportunities a year to train at Universal. Agents have toured all of the
on-site resorts, dined at all of the restaurants, enjoyed VIP Tours, and
experienced the different special events and entertainment offerings.

We are equipped to assist you in planning the perfect vacation!

Rachelle Murphy (rachelle@marvelousmousetravels.com)

Favorite Event: Halloween Horror
Nights

Rachelle has been an agent with
Marvelous Mouse Travels since May
2016. Rachelle lives in Fairhope,
Alabama and is a Universal Annual
Passholder. Universal is Rachelle's
highest selling destination! She
loves attending the different special
events at Universal! This is her favorite
vacation destination for thrilling
adventures with her kids and relaxing,
adult fun with her husband or friends! She would love to help you plan
your next family or adult adventure!

Jodie Graham (jodie.graham@marvelousmousetravels.com)

Favorite Restaurant: Toadstool Cafe

Jodie has been an agent with Marvelous Mouse Travels since May 2017. Jodie lives in Charlotte, North Carolina and is a Universal Annual Passholder. Universal is Jodie's highest selling destination! She enjoys visiting the parks frequently with her daughters to experience all of the seasonal activities and events, especially The Holidays! While she loves to spend a lot of time at the parks, she also enjoys relaxing at the resorts and enjoying the amenities and time at the pool. Jodie cannot wait to help you plan your Universal vacation!

Chelsea Hart (chelsea@marvelousmousetravels.com)

Favorite Ride: Studio Tour

Chelsea has been an agent with Marvelous Mouse Travels since 2016. Even though she lives in Queens, New York, she still makes good use of her Universal Annual Pass with multiple visits each year. She is a HUGE Harry Potter fan, but her favorite part of Universal Hollywood is the Backlot Studio Tour! She loves planning Universal vacations for her clients and getting to share in their excitement!

Dominica Fenstermacher (dominica@marvelousmousetravels.com)

Favorite Ride: The Mummy Returns

Dominica has been an agent with Marvelous Mouse Travels since 2022. She lives in southern California. She is an annual passholder at Universal Studios Hollywood and has been since she was a kid. She enjoys spending the day in the parks or just running in for a quick ride and lunch! As an avid movie watcher, her favorite thing is seeing the stories she loves come to life! The Studio Tour truly puts you in the movies! New or seasoned travelers, there is always something for everyone!

Jenna Konkel (jenna@marvelousmousetravels.com)

Favorite Event: The Holidays

Jenna has been an agent with Marvelous Mouse Travel since July 2018. She moved to Florida from Wisconsin in 2016 specifically for the theme park fun and has been a Universal Orlando Annual Passholder ever since! Universal theme parks are her first choice for date nights, vacations, and entertainment, especially during The Holidays!

Sonya D'Aulerio (sonya@marvelousmousetravels.com)

Favorite Universal Partner Hotel: The Garland

Sonya has been an agent with Marvelous Mouse Travels since 2016. She lives in the Philadelphia suburbs but enjoys visiting Universal Studios on both coasts! She loves attending the special events, especially Halloween Horror Nights and The Holidays. She is a thrill seeker who loves roller coasters, Jurassic Park, and Harry Potter.
Sonya looks forward to helping you plan an amazing Universal vacation!

Quinn Lacy (quinn@marvelousmousetravels.com)

Favorite Ride: Studio Tour

Quinn joined Marvelous Mouse Travels in 2020. She has been vacationing to Universal Orlando Resort since they opened in 1990. At any time throughout the year, you will find her enjoying various holidays and special events at Universal. She is not only a self-proclaimed thrill ride junkie, but she is also an avid Harry Potter fan and will proudly wear her house colors of Blue and Bronze... Team Ravenclaw!

10

Molly Davis (molly@marvelousmousetravels.com)

Favorite Ride: Mario Kart: Bowser's Challenge

Molly has been an agent with Marvelous Mouse Travels since 2017. She lives in Orlando, Florida and visits Universal Orlando weekly. She is a huge Universal theme park fan. She loves Universal Studios Hollywood because it offers something for everyone of all ages. Whether you are a Harry Potter fan, adrenaline junkie, or just looking for a quick getaway, Universal is a top destination to visit.

Molly looks forward to helping you plan your future Universal vacation!

Jaclyn Vercillo (Jaclyn.vercillo@marvelousmousetravels.com)

Favorite Ride: Jurassic World

Jaclyn joined Marvelous Mouse Travels in 2017. She lives in Los Angeles and is a big theme park foodie, always on the hunt for something new to try. When she is not hunting down the latest treat, you will find her taking a ride on the World Famous Studio Tour. Universal Studios Hollywood is her home base and she puts her annual pass to good use!

Brittany Lapicki (brittany.lapicki@marvelousmousetravels.com)

Favorite Ride: Jurassic World

Brittany has been an agent with Marvelous Mouse Travels since September 2018. Brittany has been going to Universal Orlando and Hollywood since 1990 and has been an Annual Passholder for over 20 years. Universal is one of her favorite destinations because of the amazing rides, nightlife, unique resorts, and memories she creates with her friends and family.
Brittany looks forward to helping you with your vacation planning needs!

Jennifer Travis (Jennifer.Travis@marvelousmousetravels.com)

Favorite Ride: Studio Tour

Jen has been a travel agent with Marvelous Mouse Travels since April 2021. She originally grew up in Massachusetts, however, she currently lives in northern Virginia. Jen's heart belongs to the spellbinding allure of both Universal Studios Hollywood and Universal Orlando Resort. With her friends and family, Jen has embarked on countless escapades, weaving the fabric of unforgettable memories at Universal since 2005. She is a Universal Annual Passholder, and the park's special events have become one of her favorite destinations for excitement including Halloween Horror Nights. Whether you're yearning for an adults only escape or a magical family getaway, Jen is your dedicated theme park guide!

WHY BOOK WITH A MARVELOUS MOUSE TRAVELS' AGENT

If you are visiting Universal Studios Hollywood for the first time, ready to plan your next adventure, or have already booked and need additional help, let Marvelous Mouse Travels be there to support and guide you! To connect with a Universal expert, contact www.marvelousmousetravels.com/contactus.

There are so many great reasons why you should use a Marvelous Mouse Travels' agent to book your next Universal Studios Hollywood vacation. If you have already booked and want to transfer your reservation to Marvelous Mouse Travels, you can do that too!

OUR SERVICES ARE FREE

There is never an additional cost to use a Marvelous Mouse Travels' agent. It is the *same* price to book with a MMT agent as it is to book direct. However, when you book your vacation directly with Universal, you are paying for a service that you are not receiving. If you book with Marvelous Mouse Travels, you have an expert guiding you throughout the entire process. Your agent can be as involved with the planning process as you want.

FIRSTHAND EXPERIENCE

Marvelous Mouse Travels has agents frequently visiting the parks. Whether on a personal trip or at an on-site Universal training, our knowledge and expertise is invaluable. We will help guide you when booking and planning your next Universal vacation. As the Top Travel Agency, our tips to share are one-of-a-kind and will help you plan the best vacation possible. All agents also complete Universal's Partner Community training annually to stay up to date on all important updates and information.

PROBLEM SOLVING

Your agent is there to answer any questions you have before, during, and even after your trip! If you run into any problems during your vacation, your agent can handle it or give guidance on the best course of action. Why would you not want someone to help you handle any issues that may arise, so you can quickly get back to enjoying your getaway?

YOUR OWN PERSONAL CONCIERGE

Have a question? Your agent will have an answer for you. If they do not know, they have the combined knowledge of about 300 agents to ask. Looking for a great nearby restaurant to enjoy? Your MMT agent can give recommendations and even make your dining reservations for you (if required). If you have a problem, want to apply a promotion to your reservation, or need additional help, your trusty travel agent can contact Universal Studios on your behalf! This could save you hours on the phone!

CHANGING POLICIES

Agents are up-to-date on any change in policies. Staying informed about safety protocols and other key guidelines is important, as rules in the park can change at any moment.

STRATEGIES AND TIPS

Your travel agent can help provide you with the best strategies for navigating the park and nearby areas and experiences. Agents have tips and tricks to help you make the most out of your Universal Studios vacation. Your agent will learn your likes and needs and plan the perfect trip for you and your friends or family. We do all the work… You have all the fun!

SUPPORTING A SMALL BUSINESS

When you book through a Marvelous Mouse Travels' agent, you are supporting a small business and receiving the benefit of one-on-one attention and support. Think of us as your friend that will make sure your Universal vacation is relaxing, enjoyable, and memorable!

Ready for Marvelous Mouse Travels to help you plan your next Universal Studios Hollywood vacation? Contact us today at www.marvelousmousetravels.com/contactus.

PREPARE FOR YOUR TRIP

There are so many ways to plan a trip to Universal Studios Hollywood! Not only is a day or two in the parks such a memorable experience, but you can also add more adventure in the surrounding areas for even more fun!

TICKETS

There are a few different ticket options available to guests. Ticket pricing is date-based, so the pricing will fluctuate throughout the year. With Universal, ages 10 and older are considered an adult and ages 3-9 are considered a child. Children two and under will receive free admission.

Your ticket gives you access to all rides, shows, parades, shops, food service locations, and seasonal offerings such Lunar New Year and The Holidays! You can purchase your tickets through your Marvelous Mouse Travels' agent who will provide you with a booking confirmation that has a barcode that you present at the gate. You do not need to stop at a ticket booth line.

1-Day Admission: Starting at $109 (plus tax) or 2-Day Admission: Starting at $159 (plus tax)

The second day of admission must be used within seven days of the first day of admission unless there is a special ticket offer that specifies otherwise.

There are also the Hollywood Plus Passes that give you access to the theme park fun plus your choice of activities in the surrounding areas! Choose between a Hollywood Plus 3 Pass or Hollywood Plus 5 Pass and have access to both Universal Studios Hollywood and your choice of the following attractions: Academy Museum of Motion Picture, Aquarium of the Pacific*, Autry Museum of the American West, Citadel Outlets, The Grammy Museum, L.A. Zoo, Madame Tussauds Hollywood*, Starline City Sightseeing Evening Tour, Starline City Sightseeing Los Angeles, Hop On – Hop Off, Starline Celebrity Homes Tour, Starline Hollywood Walking Tour, Sofi Stadium Tour*, TLC Chinese Theatre, and Warner Bros. Studio Tour*.

The experiences with an asterisk (*) require advanced reservations. At the time you activate your pass, the remaining attraction redemptions are available and must be used within seven days. Parking is not included.

Your Hollywood Plus Pass must also be registered through the "SmartVisit" App. After registering, you will be able to activate and retrieve your individual digital pass(es) utilizing the 28-digit human readable code. With the App you can view the details of the attractions including location, maps, opening times, helpful tips, and make reservations where required!

SUPER NINTENDO WORLD EARLY ACCESS TICKET

Wanting to get a head start to your day with Hollywood's newest attraction? Add the Super Nintendo World Early Access Ticket to your reservation, and get inside the theme park an hour before opening to enjoy this brand new and immersive world! Pricing starts at $20 per person.

ANNUAL PASSES

There are various Annual Passes available including Platinum Annual Pass, Gold Annual Pass, Silver Annual Pass, and California Neighbor Pass. Platinum Annual Passes have no blackout dates and include other perks such as free Halloween Horror Nights ticket, Universal Express access after 3:00 PM, free general parking, etc. Gold Annual Passes allows guests to visit for 325 days and includes other benefits such as 15% off merchandise and food, free general parking, etc. Silver Annual Pass allows guests to visit 275 days and includes perks such as invitations to special events, discounted park tickets and Halloween Horror Nights tickets, etc. California Neighbor Passes are for California residents and allows guests to visit over 150 days of the year and includes the same benefits as the Silver Annual Pass.

UNIVERSAL STUDIOS HOLLYWOOD UNIVERSAL EXPRESS TICKET

Get to the fun faster with Universal's Express Ticket! The Universal Express Ticket includes your park admission AND one time, per day access to each ride including Mario Kart: Bowsers Challenge, attraction, and seated show, and one-time, per day reservation-free entry into SUPER NINTENDO WORLD when reservations are required to enter the land. Express pass lanes are separate and shorter queues than standby. Your Universal Express Ticket can be purchased through your Marvelous Mouse Travels' agent, and once your barcoded booking confirmation is scanned at the main gate, they will provide you with an express pass ticket! Pricing starts at $199 (plus tax).

UNIVERSAL STUDIOS HOLLYWOOD EXPRESS UNLIMITED TICKET

Get to the fun faster with Universal's Express Ticket! The Universal Express Ticket includes your park admission AND unlimited access to each ride including Mario Kart: Bowsers Challenge, attraction, and seated show, and one-time, per day reservation-free entry into SUPER NINTENDO WORLD when reservations are required to enter the land. Express pass lanes are separate and shorter queues than standby. You can purchase an Express Ticket with your Marvelous Mouse Travel agent and upgrade inside the park to unlimited express. Pricing starts at $239 (plus tax).

UNIVERSAL STUDIOS HOLLYWOOD VIP EXPERIENCE

Experience Universal Hollywood like a VIP! Select your preferred date and time and enjoy VIP privileges and Express unlimited access to rides, attractions (including the backlot) and seated shows with your expert tour guide! You will begin your day in the exclusive VIP lounge with a light breakfast before starting your adventure into the parks. For lunch, you will be treated to a gourmet buffet at Moulin Rouge prepared for you by Universal's very own executive chef. Plus, theme park admission, complimentary valet parking, and VIP entry to the theme park are also included with your experience! Pricing starts at $369 (plus tax).

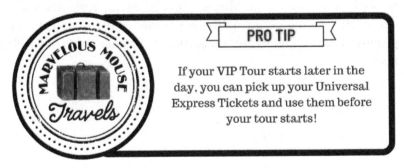

PRO TIP

If your VIP Tour starts later in the day, you can pick up your Universal Express Tickets and use them before your tour starts!

ADDITIONAL TOURS

We can add even more memorable experiences to your visit to Universal Hollywood by adding a "A Day in LA" tour or Warner Brothers Studio Tour!

From your Universal Studios Hollywood partner resort, enjoy a complimentary pick up to spend your day exploring Los Angeles, Venice Beach, Santa Monica, Beverly Hills, and Hollywood on the "A Day in LA" tour. So many exciting places you will visit throughout your tour including the world-famous pier in Santa Monica, Rodeo Drive, the sunset strip, Hollywood Walk of Fame, Hollywood sign, and more! These tours are a full day experience, stopping for a period of time at each destination, in an air conditioned vehicle with a knowledgeable guide. Private tours are also available. This tour can be added to your Universal vacation package.

The Warner Brothers Studio Tour cannot be included with your Universal Studios Hollywood vacation package, however, this is a very popular tour in the area. On this studio tour, you will go behind the camera to see how the magic of movies and television is made. You will explore sets from various television shows and movies, view props and costumes used by action stars, experience fun photo opportunities, and more! For a longer and even more immersive experience, you can upgrade to a Studio Tour Plus! This Tour is also included with the Hollywood Plus Pass. Let your Marvelous Mouse Travels' agent assist you with booking this experience with your Universal Hollywood vacation!

AIRPORT TRANSPORTATION
For a visit to Universal Studios Hollywood, guests can fly into four nearby airports: Hollywood Burbank Airport (4 miles away), Los Angeles International Airport (14 miles away), Long Beach Airport (25 miles away), and Santa Ana Airport (42.7 miles away).

Universal offers one-way transportation by sedan, SUV, or van to/from Hollywood Burbank Airport that can be added to your vacation package.

From Los Angeles International Airport, you can take a train from Union Station in LA! Using your Metrolink ticket, you would transfer to the Red Line Metro Rail subway, head westbound, and exit at Universal City/Studio City! From there, you would take a free shuttle to the front gate of Universal Studios Hollywood! The shuttles run every 10-15 minutes, seven days a week, 7:00 A.M. until two hours after park closing! In addition, guests can choose to use various bus services, rent a car, or use a rideshare like Lyft or Uber. Due to the heavy traffic presence in Los Angeles, guests may decide not to start their vacation with a stressful driving experience.

From Long Beach Airport, the least expensive option for transportation to Universal Studios Hollywood is a bus, however, there is not a bus that takes you directly to the Universal Studios/Hollywood station; this option will require multiple transfers between buses. The easiest connection would be via taxi or rideshare like Lyft or Uber. Again, renting a car is also an option.

Keep in mind that all partner hotels and Universal Studios Hollywood do charge daily/nightly parking fees for guests who choose to rent a car.

LA AREA VACATION PACKAGE
Universal Studios Hollywood offers an "LA Vacation Package" option for guests that gives you access to both the theme park and most popular experiences around Los Angeles. With this package, guests receive a 4-night hotel accommodation, 3-Attraction Hollywood Plus Pass, and A Day in LA Tour. Please see additional information about the 3-Attraction Hollywood Plus Pass above under "Tickets" and the "A Day in LA Tour" above under "Additional Tours." Your Marvelous Mouse Travels' agent can assist you with pricing and booking this amazing experience too!

HISTORY OF UNIVERSAL STUDIOS HOLLYWOOD

Universal Studios Hollywood first opened their doors to the public in 1915. At that time, the admission to enter was $.05 and included a petting zoo experience and boxed lunch. Carl Laemmle was the founder and had big plans for the space. By 1930, Universal Studios Hollywood was a full functioning film and television studio!

Big things were in the works and, by 1962, the World Famous Studio Tour opened to visitors. It was an attraction, giving guests backstage access to television and film lots and teaching them how the "magic" was created behind-the-scenes. But, by 1968, the Screen Actors Guild had enforced rules to limit the access of guests to shows and films actively shooting. Today, the Studio Tour takes you through old and new Hollywood history and has added features such as 3D experiences and simulations. Along the Studio Tour, you will see sound stages and sets from the past including *Jaws, Dracula, Creature from the Black Lagoon, Apollo 13, Back to the Future* and many other award-winning pictures. You will also see sets of recent television shows such as *Once Upon a Time in Hollywood, The Good Place, The Voice*, and *The Fabelmans.*

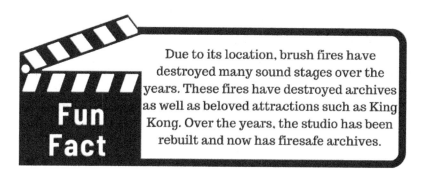

Fun Fact

Due to its location, brush fires have destroyed many sound stages over the years. These fires have destroyed archives as well as beloved attractions such as King Kong. Over the years, the studio has been rebuilt and now has firesafe archives.

In 1964, Universal Studios Hollywood was officially named a theme park, and, by 1965, the first ride, War Lord Tower opened. To this day, Universal Studios Hollywood is the world's only operating studio and theme park. It has been home to fan favorite rides and attractions like E.T., Back to the Future, King Kong, Earthquake, Jurassic Park, and Backdraft, to name a few.

By 1970, we got to see some of our beloved pets take the stage when the Animal Actors School opened to park guests. The animal actors showed off their adorable and special talents. Sadly, this show closed in 2023 to make way for a new *Fast and Furious* rollercoaster set to open in 2025. In the late 90s and early 2000s, Universal introduced more shows to their theme park. Waterworld, a live sea war spectacular, opened in 1995 and is still extremely popular today. This show will not only draw you in with the story, but you will be blown away by the stunts and special effects too!

In 1993, Universal CityWalk opened nearby, giving visitors more nightlife entertainment, restaurants, and shops to enjoy.

Fast forward to 2016, The Wizarding World of Harry Potter opened in the Upper Lot. You can now head to Hogsmeade to enjoy a butterbeer, shop for an interactive wand, experience Flight of the Hippogriff or Harry Potter and the Forbidden Journey, dine in Three Broomsticks, and more!

Most recently, in 2023, Super Nintendo World opened in the Lower Lot. Guests can now "shrink" in size to enter Mushroom Kingdom and ride Mario Kart: Bowser's Challenge, use their Power-Up Band to earn points for their Super Mario Brothers' team, meet character favorites such as Mario, Luigi, Princess Peach, and Toad, or enjoy a meal at Toadstool Cafe! This world has been a huge hit for this destination!

With all the attractions and shows, both new and old, Universal Studios Hollywood is such a fun experience for all ages and a must-do for everyone visiting California!

Universal Hollywood is separated into two sections- Upper Lot and Lower Lot. The Upper Lot includes Minion Land, Springfield USA, The Wizarding World of Harry Potter, and Production Plaza. The Lower Lot includes Super Nintendo World and select rides such as Jurassic Park, Revenge of the Mummy, and Transformers- The Ride 3D. While Super Nintendo World is briefly discussed in the Lower Lot section, this land does also have its own, more detailed section.

UPPER LOT

MINION LAND

Rides

The Secret Life of Pets: Off the Leash- Take the streets of New York City with Max, Duke, and the whole Pets crew! It's Pet Adoption Day, and everyone needs to look their best, even you! Guests will be transformed into a stray puppy and with a little bit of luck and shampoo, they will be adopted too!
- Kid Friendly
- Height Requirement- Minimum Height 34" (86.4 cm)
- Under 48" (121.9 cm)- Supervising Companion Required

- Virtual Line Available
- Universal Express Pass Accepted
- Accessibility and Restrictions- Wheelchair Accessible; No Service Animals permitted; Closed Captioning

Despicable Me Minion Mayhem- Join Gru, Agnes, Edith and Margo as you hop on the ride of your life and become an actual minion. You will dance, sing, and laugh your way throughout this once-in-a-lifetime journey. This is a kid-friendly attraction, but adults may also find this ride enjoyable!
- Kid Friendly
- Height Requirement- Minimum Height 40" (101.6 cm)
- Under 48" (121.9 cm)- Supervising Companion Required
- Universal Express Pass Accepted
- Child Swap Available
- Accessibility and Restrictions- Must transfer from wheelchair; Must transfer from ECV; Service Animals permitted; Open Captioning

Silly Swirly- Welcome to the seaside carnival from Despicable Me! Hop in your own bug and soar and swirl above the boardwalk while grooving to happy tunes!
- Kid Friendly
- No Height Requirement
- Under 48" (122 cm)- Supervising Companion Required
- Universal Express Pass Accepted
- Accessibility and Restrictions- Wheelchair and ECV Accessible; Service Animals permitted

Super Silly Fun Land- Minions unite! This area is modeled after the seaside carnival in Despicable Me. Guests have several carnival games, a dry interactive area, and a water play area with over 80 water features to enjoy!
- Kid Friendly
- Accessibility and Restrictions- Wheelchair and ECV Accessible; Service Animals permitted
- A water play/splash zone area is available in this area. Kids and adults must wear water shoes to enter. Bathing suits are highly recommended.

Dining

Minion Café- Sandwiches, Salads, Rotisserie Chicken, Pork Ramen Bowl, Macaroni and Cheese, Chicken Tenders, Nachos and a variety of desserts. Serving lunch and dinner, nonalcoholic, and alcoholic beverages.
- Quick Service dining available
- Price Range- $18.99 and under per adult
- Mobile Ordering Available
- Fan Favorite- Classic Grilled Cheese with Tomato Soup- Sharp Cheddar Cheese, Mexican blended cheese, crinkle cut fries, marinara sauce dip

Despicable Delights- Featuring *Despicable Me*-themed snacks and treats such as Churros, Cotton Candy, Nutella Banana Pudding, Soft Service Ice Cream, Minion Car Popcorn Bucket, Collectible Minion Slipper, Floats, Fountain Drinks, Bottled, Premium and Minion Boxed Water.
- Price Range- $10 and Under
- Fan Favorite- Nutella Banana Pudding- Banana pudding, vanilla wafer, Nutella, cocoa butter

City Snack Shop- Specialty Pretzels, Croissants, Cookies, Fountain Drinks, Powerade, Premium and Bottled Water, Juice, Hot Cocoa and Coffee
- Price Range- $13.99 and under
- Fan Favorite- Giant Everything Pretzel- Giant warmed and ,toasted authentic Bavarian style pretzel topped with Everything Bagel Seasoning

Shopping

Super Silly Stuff- Ride-inspired gifts such as plush minions, fluffy unicorns, apparel, and more

The Pets Store- *The Secret Life of Pets*-themed apparel, plush, toys, and souvenirs

Characters/Shows/Entertainment

Despicable Me Carnival Games- The fun never ends in Minion Land! Try your luck at one of the many fun carnival games available in this area such as Minion Toss, Minion Mishap, and Super Silly Space Killers. You never know what Minion Mayhem is in store!

SPRINGFIELD, USA

Rides

The Simpsons Ride- Join the Simpsons on this virtual reality, motion simulated "rollercoaster" as you soar through Krustyland.
- Height Requirement- Minimum Heights 40" (102 cm)
- Under 48" (122 cm): Requires Supervising Companion Required
- Universal Express Pass Accepted
- Child Swap Available
- Accessibility and Restrictions- Must transfer from wheelchair

Dining

Bumblebee Man's Taco Truck- Korean Beef, Carne Asada and Chicken Tacos, Nachos, Duff Beer, Buzz Cola, and fountain drinks. Serving lunch and dinner.
- Quick Service dining available
- Price Range- $15.99 and under per adult
- Fan Favorite- Tacos Carne Asada- Tender marinated grilled beef **served in soft corn tortillas with onion and cilantro**

Cletus' Chicken Shack- Fried Chicken Platter, Chicken Tenders, Chicken and Waffle Sandwich, Grilled Chicken Sandwich, Chicken Caesar Salad, Fries and Desserts. Serving lunch, dinner, Duff Beer, Buzz Cola, and other various fountain drinks, beer, and nonalcoholic beverages.
- Quick service dining available
- Price Range- $16.99 and under per adult
- Mobile Ordering Available
- Fan Favorite- Chicken and Waffle Sandwich- Fried chicken breast and waffles with lettuce, tomato, maple mayo sauce, and fries

Duff Brewery Beer Garden- Draft Beer, Cocktails, Blended Drinks and Wine. Serving daily.
- Price Range- $16 and under
- Fan Favorite- Dufftoberfest

Krusty Burger- Burgers, Ribwich, Footlong Hot Dog, and Chicken Caesar Salad. Serving lunch, dinner, draft beer, cider, fountain drinks, juice, bottled and premium water, milkshakes, and squishee.
- Quick service dining available
- Price Range- $16.99 and under per adult
- Mobile Ordering Available
- Fan Favorite- Krusty Burger- ⅓ lb patty with secret sauce, American cheese, lettuce, tomato, and pickles

Lard Lad Donuts- Donuts, Specialty Coffees, fountain drinks, and a variety of other beverages
- Price Range- $9.99 and under
- Mobile Ordering Available
- Fan Favorite- The Big Pink- Lard Lad's famous giant donut with sweet creamy frosting and sprinkles (made fresh daily)

Luigi's Pizza and Pasta- Pizza, Pasta, Chicken Caesar Salad, and Desserts. Serving lunch and dinner, draft beer, fountain drinks, and various beverages.
- Quick Service dining available
- Price Range- $14.99 and under per adult
- Mobile Ordering Available
- Fan Favorite- Fat Tony's Meatball Marinara Witness-Protected Pasta- Penne pasta with marinara sauce and meatballs

Moe's Tavern- Cocktails, Blended Drinks, Wine and Draft Beer. Serving daily.
- Price Range- $16 and under
- Fan Favorite- Blackberry Mule- Blackberry liquor, vodka, ginger beer, and lime juice

Shopping

Kwik-E-Mart- Simpsons merchandise, Duff Beer, Lard Lad Donuts, souvenirs, and toys

Characters/Shows/Entertainment

The Simpsons Carnival Games- Step right up for some carnival style fun! Make your way over to Krustyland to test your skills in Springfield's very own favorites such as The Full Nelson, Dunk or Flunk with Principal Skinner, Sideshow You, Thar She Throws, Wild and Willie, and more!

THE WIZARDING WORLD OF HARRY POTTER

Rides

Flight of the Hippogriff- This family-friendly rollercoaster features the magical creature, Hippogriff, and takes you on an exciting journey around Hagrid's Hut and the pumpkin patch.
- Kid Friendly
- Height Requirement- Minimum Height 39" (99 cm)
- Under 48" (121.9 cm)- Supervising Companion Required
- Universal Express Pass Accepted

- Accessibility and Restrictions- Must transfer from wheelchair; Wheelchair Accessible

Harry Potter and the Forbidden Journey- With just a flick of a wand and a little bit of magic, you will soar above Hogwarts with Harry Potter and friends!
- Height Requirement- Minimum Height 48" (122 cm)
- Universal Express Pass Accepted
- Child Swap Available
- Single Rider Available
- Accessibility and Restrictions- Must transfer from wheelchair; Wheelchair Accessible

Dining

Hog's Head- Draft beer and Butterbeer

- Price Range- $16 and under
- Fan Favorite- Hogs Head Bite- equal parts Ale and Hard Cider

Magic Neep Cart- Fresh fruit, cold beverages, bottles beers, and snacks

Three Broomsticks- Traditional English dishes including Traditional English Breakfast among other favorites- "The Great Feast," Fish and Chips, Shepherd's Pie, Bangers and Mash, fresh vegetables, and desserts. Serving breakfast, lunch and dinner, nonalcoholic, and alcoholic beverages.
- Quick Service dining available
- Price Range- Breakfast $16.99 and under per adult / Lunch and Dinner $19.99 and under per adult
- Mobile Ordering Available
- Fan Favorite- Breakfast- Traditional English Breakfast- Fresh scrambled eggs, sausage link, bacon, ham, baked beans, baked tomato, sauteed mushrooms, and potatoes served with a butter croissant and black pudding / Dinner- Bangers and Mash- Grilled English sausage, creamy mashed potatoes, roasted tomatoes, sautéed onions and cabbage, and minted peas and gravy

Shopping

Dervish & Bangers- Apparel, Toys, Souvenirs, Collectibles, Gifts, Jewelry

Filch's Emporium of Confiscated Goods- Banned items such as the Marauder's Map, Wizard's Chess, magical creatures, and more

Gladrags Wizardwear- Authentic Hogwarts robes, house-specific attire, and jewelry

Honeydukes- Sweets including Cauldron Cakes and Fizzing Whizzbees

Ollivanders- Interactive wands

Owl Post- Stationery, quills, stamps, ink, and owl-related souvenirs

Characters/Shows/Entertainment

Ollivanders- Interactive wand-choosing experience.

Triwizard Spirit Rally- The largest wizarding schools in Europe- Hogwarts, Durmstrang, and Beauxbatons- compete in the Triwizard Tournament. During this rally, you will be entertained with the skills each school brings to the tournament! Stay after the performance for a photo opportunity with some of the students from Durmstrang and Beauxbatons!

Frog Choir- Enjoy a small musical ensemble of Hogwarts students performing familiar wizarding songs with their large croaking frogs. Each of the students in the ensemble represent one of four houses.

The Nighttime Lights at Hogwarts Castle- Celebrate the four houses, as they are magically brought to life in a stunning display of lights and music! Watch the castle transform as projections make their way across the majestic Hogwarts Castle!

Dark Arts at Hogwarts Castle- On select nights in the Fall, watch in amazement as Dementors, Death Eaters, and other creatures of the darkness take over Hogwarts Castle. Be dazzled as the castle is wrapped in sinister images and a magical display of light and music! (Check Special Events for more information.)

PRODUCTION PLAZA

Rides

DreamWorks Theatre Featuring Kung Fu Panda- Master Po needs your help! This 4D adventure will have you on a journey of awesomeness, as you deliver the liquid of ultimate power to the Emperor.
Kid Friendly
- No Height Requirement
- Universal Express Pass Accepted
- Accessibility and Restrictions- Must transfer from wheelchair; Wheelchair Accessible

Dining

Cocina Mexicana- Tacos, Burritos, Nachos, Taco Salad, Desserts, Specialty Coffee and Teas, Frappe, and fountain beverages. Serving lunch and dinner, nonalcoholic, and alcoholic beverages.
- Quick Service dining available
- Price Range- $14.99 and under per adult
- Mobile Ordering Available
- Fan Favorite- Sopes- Refried beans, pico de gallo, Spanish rice, and guacamole with a choice of chicken or carnitas

French Street Bistro- Artisan Sandwiches, Wraps, Quiche, Gourmet Salads, Pastries, and a selection of grab-and-go items. Serving lunch and dinner.
- Quick Service dining available
- Price Range- $13.99 and under per adult
- Fan Favorite- Chicken Bánh Mì- Teriyaki chicken served on french bread with mushrooms, carrots, beets, jalapenos, and cilantro topped with vegan sriracha mayonnaise

Hollywood & Dine- Sandwiches, Burgers, Salads, Corn Dogs, Funnel Cake, and other Desserts.   Serving lunch and dinner, nonalcoholic, and alcoholic beverages.
- Quick Service dining available
- Price Rance- $17.99 and under per adult
- Mobile Ordering Available
- Fan Favorite- Summer Strawberry Salad- Mixed greens, radish, cherry tomatoes, red onion, goat cheese, and fresh strawberries tossed in a strawberry vinaigrette and topped with croutons

Mulligan's Irish Pub- International and Domestic Beers, Spirits, and Snacks
- Price Range- $16 and under
- Fan Favorite- Guinness Old Fashioned- Old Forester, Guinness Stout, spiced bitters, simple syrup, and maraschino cherry

Palace Deli & Market- Sandwiches, Salads, Hot Grab-and-Go Entrees, Famous Turkey Leg, Rotisserie Chicken, Seasonal Soups, Fresh Fruit, Snacks, and Desserts. Serving lunch and dinner, nonalcoholic, and alcoholic beverages.
- Quick Service dining available
- Price Range- $14.99 and under per adult
- Fan Favorite- California Roll- Served with ginger and wasabi

Mel's Diner- Burgers, Hot Dogs, Sandwiches, Fries, Onion Rings, Milkshakes, Funnel Cake, Brownies, Retro-Inspired Dishes such as Fried Chicken Combo and Meatloaf Combo (On special occasions). Serving lunch and dinner, draft beer, cocktails, fountain drinks, and other various beverages.
- Quick Service dining available
- Price Range- $19.64 and under per adult
- Mobile Ordering Available
- Fan Favorite- Mel's Classic Burger- American Cheese, lettuce, tomato, pickles, and thousand island dressing on a toasted bun with crinkle cut fries.

Shopping

Feature Presentation Store- Super Nintendo World merchandise

Universal Studio Store- Apparel, candy, souvenirs, toys, collectibles

Characters/Shows/Entertainment

WaterWorld- Be sure to experience Universal Hollywood's #1 rated show! Soak up incredible stunts, firefighting, and an explosion of events including twist and turns that will keep you on the edge of your seat!

Celebrate with DreamWorks' Trolls- DreamWorks' Trolls are back! Meet Guy Diamond, Poppy, and Branch in their new home full of glitter and glam!

Upper Lot Character Sightings

Whether you find your favorites wandering near the park entrance or in their respective lands, you are sure to meet at least a few of your favorites, such as:

- Beetlejuice
- Dracula
- Curious George
- Scooby Doo and the Gang
- SpongeBob SquarePants
- Gru, the girls, and Minions
- Marilyn Monroe
- Betty Boop
- Shrek
- King Julian

Character appearances are subject to change. Ask any park employee about character appearance times and locations.

Now, let's head over to the Lower Lot to learn about the character sightings, dining options, and rides that are available there for you to experience!

LOWER LOT

The most popular feature of the Lower Lot is the brand new Super Nintendo World, but there is still so much to see and experience inside of this area including multiple rides, dining locations, and shops!

Rides

Jurassic World- The Ride- Enjoy a nice float through Jurassic World where you will encounter the Mosasaurus and other dinosaurs from the beloved franchise. But, be on the lookout because the Idominus Rex has escaped and is hungry...
- Height Requirement- Minimum Height 42" (106.7 cm)
- Universal Express Pass Accepted
- Child Swap Available
- Ride Photo Opportunity
- Lockers Available
- Single Rider Available
- Accessibility and Restrictions- Must transfer from wheelchair; Wheelchair Accessible; Open Captioning

Revenge of The Mummy-The Ride- Fleeing the evil Imhotep, some surprises await you on this rollercoaster in the dark. Don't worry about screaming… No one will hear you!
- Height Requirement- Minimum Height 48" (122 cm)
- Universal Express Pass Accepted
- Child Swap Available
- Ride Photo Opportunity
- Lockers Available
- Single Rider Available
- Accessibility and Restrictions- Must transfer from wheelchair; Wheelchair Accessible; Open Captioning

Transformers- The Ride 3D- Join Optimus Prime and Bumblebee in the ultimate 3D/4D battle to defeat Megatron and save planet Earth.
- Height Requirement- Minimum Height 40" (102 cm)
- Under 48" (121.9 cm)- Supervising Companion Required
- Universal Express Pass Accepted
- Child Swap Available
- Ride Photo Opportunity
- Lockers Available
- Single Rider Available
- Accessibility and Restrictions- Must transfer from wheelchair; Wheelchair Accessible; Open Captioning

Dining

Jurassic Cafe- Pizzas, Sandwiches, Spaghetti and Meatballs, Caesar Salads, and Fettuccine Alfredo. Serving snacks, lunch, dinner, alcoholic, and non-alcoholic beverages.
- Quick Service dining available
- Price Range- $19.99 and under per adult
- Mobile Ordering Available
- Fan Favorite- Raptor Leg- served with fries

Mummy Eats- Classic Corn Dogs, Spicy Corn Dogs, Korean Corn Dogs, Vegetarian Corn Dogs, Churro and Chips. Serving lunch, dinner, alcoholic, and non-alcoholic beverages.
- Quick Service dining available
- Price Range- $12.49 and under per adult
- Fan Favorite- Vegetarian Dog- plant-based hotdog

Panda Express- Asian favorites such as Orange Chicken, Kung Pao Chicken, Egg Rolls, Beef Broccoli, Rice, Beijing Beef, Chow Mein, Cream Cheese Rangoons, and Fried Rice. Serving lunch, dinner, alcoholic, and non-alcoholic beverages.
- Quick Service dining available
- Price Range- $15.99 and under per adult
- Mobile Ordering Available
- Fan Favorite- Orange Chicken and Broccoli Beef- Broccoli beef and orange chicken with fried rice or chow mein

Studio Cafe- Sandwiches, Salads, Sushi, Wraps, Bánh Mì, Pizza, Smoked Turkey Legs, Charcuterie, Pesto Pasta Side Salad, Protein Box, Yogurt Parfait. Chips, Popcorn, Donuts, Ice Cream, and a variety of other desserts. Serving lunch, dinner, alcoholic, and non-alcoholic beverages.
- Quick Service dining available
- Price Range- $13.99 and under per adult
- Mobile Ordering Available
- Fan Favorite- Asian PrChopped Salad- Lettuce, snow peas, mandarins, cabbage, green onions and cilantro with sesame dressing.

Isla Nu-Bar- Cocktails, Blended Drinks, Wine and Draft Beer. Serving daily.
- Price Range- $21.00 and under per adult
- Fan Favorite- Ti Peach- Spiced and coconut rum mixed with bitters, lime juice. and peach puree.

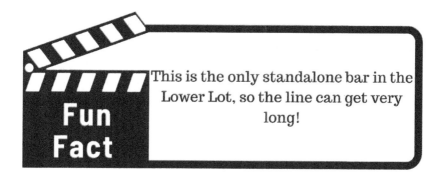

Fun Fact: This is the only standalone bar in the Lower Lot, so the line can get very long!

Starbucks- Coffee, Tea, Sandwiches, Breakfast Wraps, Croissants, Protein Box, Yogurt Parfait, Chips, and a variety of other desserts. Serving breakfast, lunch, dinner, and non-alcoholic beverages.
- Quick Service dining available
- Mobile Ordering Available
- Fan Favorite- Pink Drink

Studio Scoop- Sundaes, Ice Cream, Sodas, Hot Chocolate, Milkshakes and Water. Serving daily.
- Quick Service dining available
- Price Range- $11 and under per adult
- Fan Favorite- S'mores and More Milkshake- Chocolate milkshake topped with graham cracker crumbs, chocolate shavings, fresh whipped cream, brownie wedges, and chocolate syrup

Shopping

Animation Studio Store- Animation fans unite! This cool store is filled with animation merchandise that includes, but not limited to, Scooby Doo, Sanrio, DreamWorks Animation, and Illumination Entertainment.

Character Shop- This is your one stop shop for all things Super Nintendo! You will find figurines, collectables, apparel, and other unique items.

Jurrassic Outfitters- You can't leave Universal Hollywood without commemorating your visit to Jurassic World! Check out this shop for collectables, pins, jewel, apparel, sweet treats and more.

Transformers Supply Vault- A small shop of everything Transformers including comic books, figurines, clothes, toys, and more!

SUPER NINTENDO WORLD

Mario Kart: Bowser's Challenge- Grab your Power-Up bands and strap on your special goggles, as you try to defeat the evil Bowser in Mario Kart to win the Golden Cup. Each experience is different so make sure to ride several times!
- Height Requirement- Minimum Height 40" (102 cm)
- Under 48" (121.9 cm)- Supervising Companion Required
- Universal Express Pass Accepted
- Child Swap Available
- Ride Photo Opportunity

- Lockers Available
- Single Rider Available
- Accessibility and Restrictions- Must transfer from wheelchair; Wheelchair Accessible; Open Captioning

Dining

Popcorn and Drink Cart- Cream Soda, Popcorn and Beverages. Serving lunch, dinner, alcoholic, and non-alcoholic beverages.
- Price Range- $39.99 and under per adult
- Fan Favorite- Mario's Strawberry Soda

Toadstool Cafe- Mario Burger, Piranha Plant Caprese, Super Mushroom Bowl, Grilled Chicken, Short Ribs, Tiramisu, and other yummy treats. Serving lunch, dinner and non-alcoholic beverages. Adorably themed restaurant with decorative seating and animation along the walls!
- Price Range- $24.99 and under per adult
- Fan Favorite- Fire Flower Spaghetti and Meatballs- Spaghetti with meatballs and mushroom marinara sauce with parsley and parmesan cheese.

Shopping

1-UP Factory- This is the place to be if you want to grab your interaction bands and other neat items for your ride on Mario Kart: Bowser's Challenge!

Characters/Shows/Entertainment

Meet Mario and Friends- Meet Mario, Luigi, Princess Peach and Toad

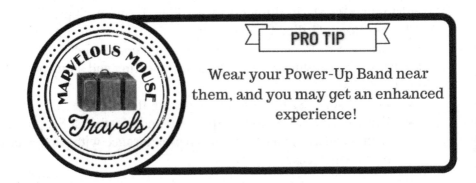

PRO TIP

Wear your Power-Up Band near them, and you may get an enhanced experience!

While a much smaller area from the Upper Lot, guests flock to this area of the park due to the popularity of the rides that are located here! So, be sure to head here early in the morning to experience this amazing section without the higher wait times and crowds!

SUPER NINTENDO WORLD HOLLYWOOD

The newest attraction area at Universal Studios Hollywood is one that is for the Nintendo fans in your travel party! Super Nintendo World opened in early 2023 and has been an extremely popular area with guests! The best part, this world is included with your admission ticket! During peak seasons, however, reservations are required to enter. One way to secure entry into Super Nintendo World is by adding an Early Access Ticket to your reservation.

This immersive world is located on the Lower Lot adjacent to the Transformers- The Ride 3D. Before launching into Super Nintendo World, make sure to buy everyone in your party a Power-Up Band, so you can all interact with the different areas to earn coins and keys and compete in challenges! At the entrance, there is a great photo opportunity to take of yourself inside a Super Mario warp pipe! After your picture, you will travel through a tunnel, taking from inside Universal Studios Hollywood into the world of Super Nintendo! You are now inside Mushroom Kingdom, greeted by the mushrooms of Toad Land, Princess Peach's Castle, Bowser's Castle, and so much more!

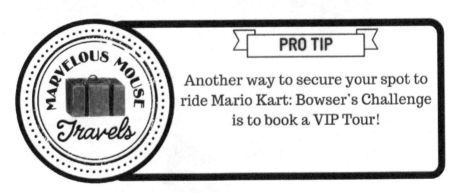

PRO TIP

Another way to secure your spot to ride Mario Kart: Bowser's Challenge is to book a VIP Tour!

Located throughout the world are different Power-Up locations. Just like in the games, you can smash yellow question mark cubes to earn coins. You will want to link your Power-Up bands to your My Universal App, so that you can track your coin and key collection progress. You can compete with other guests individually or as a team. As a team, you will be paired with all guests with the same Power-Up band for the day!

There are also multiple character meet-and-greets. Mario and Luigi will meet you in the middle of the World, under the large mushroom. If you are wearing your Power-Up band, you may get an enhanced experience! Princess Peach will be waiting for you in her pink gazebo. Toad will be available for photo and meet-and-greet experiences on the right side once you enter the World. You can find a schedule of the character meet-and-greets in your My Universal App. These characters say phrases from the video game!

Toad is also cooking some amazing food options for you at Toadstool Cafe. Enjoy an array of Toad's special burgers, Star salads, and themed treats. The food that Toad has created deserves a photo shoot, so make sure you take the time to snap your pictures! Reservations are required, and can be made through your My Universal App.

The main attraction inside Super Nintendo World is Mario Kart: Bowser's Challenge. This interactive ride is your own Mario Kart experience, launching bananas and turtle shells while you try to beat Bowser. The queue for this ride is extremely immersive and takes you through the different worlds inside of the Mario and Luigi games. You will make stops in the gem forest, Mushroom Kingdom, sky clouds, and the interior of Bowser's Castle.

Once you have traversed the queue, you will be greeted in the racing room to prepare for a Mario Kart race. This ride does require the use of a headset that looks like Mario's hat. If you or your guests do not enjoy the use of interactive goggles, this may be a ride to skip.

Mario Kart: Bowser's Challenge does have a height requirement of 40 inches, and anyone under 48 inches must be accompanied by a supervision companion. This ride also offers ride swap for groups with members that are not tall enough or do not wish to ride. A single rider queue is also offered. As of June 2024, Universal Studios Hollywood has added an Express Lane for this ride, significantly reducing wait times for anyone with a Universal Express Pass!

Universal Studios Hollywood also just added an interactive game area called the Frosted Glacier inside Super Nintendo World. In this interactive game area, you will begin by punching the "?" block, and one of four Power-Up items- Fire Flower, Ice Flower, Super Mushroom, or Super Star- will appear on the screen. You can then tap the Power-Up item, and use it, by swiping or tapping, to defeat Goombas and Red and Green Koopa Paratroopas. Also, tapping the flashing brick blocks earns you coins! The goal is to collect as many points as possible before the timed activity concludes.

After your adventures with Mario and friends, make your way through the exit tunnel, and be sure to stop at the 1-UP Factory to get all of your favorite Nintendo merchandise! Grab a Yoshi to take home, backpacks, clothing, an extra Power-Up band, candy, and so much more!

WORLD FAMOUS STUDIO TOUR

Universal Studios Hollywood is famous for its Studio Tour. This attraction is what sets Universal apart from other theme parks since it is also a film and television production studio. The tour will take you through live working sets from the golden era of filming to present day. This attraction is arguably the fan favorite.

First, you will grab a pair of 3D glasses, board your tram, and begin your tour around various lots. Jimmy Fallon will be your virtual tour guide; you will also have a Universal expert on board to give fun facts and television and film history. Recently, the Studio Tour was updated for its 60th anniversary, so you will see more video cameos from television and film stars from the most iconic Universal sets.

During your tour, you will travel between working sound stages where current shows like The Voice and Bel-Air are filming; your guide will point out sets from shows in the past such as ER, Scrubs, and the A-Team. You will also see the production offices. These offices are where the work begins to bring television shows and films to life!

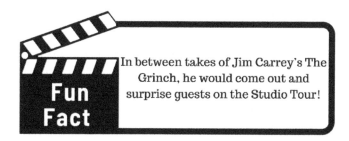

Fun Fact

In between takes of Jim Carrey's The Grinch, he would come out and surprise guests on the Studio Tour!

You will also experience a few amazing attractions during the tour! King Kong 360 3D will take you into Skull Island and require your 3D glasses. This attraction replaced the original King Kong attraction that had an animatronic, King Kong, with "banana breath"... You read that right! Unfortunately, this attraction burned down in 2008 from a wildfire in California.

You will get to visit Amity Island. This town has a small problem- a shark terrorizing the waters and eating humans! But, don't worry, this shark on the tour is mechanical and can't hurt you!

If this is your first time to California, the tour may also be your first time experiencing an earthquake on the newly refurbished attraction, "Earthquake-The Big One." On this ride, you will experience a magnitude 8.3 earthquake!!

And, as if an earthquake wasn't a wild enough experience, hold on tight for the newest attraction in the Studio Tour, "Fast and Furious-Supercharged!" Here, you will experience a high speed chase with the Fast and Furious team guiding you to the finish line.

Another unique part of the tour is visiting the outdoor sets for movies and shows such as Wisteria Lane from *Desperate Housewives*, Norman Bates at the *Bates Motel*, the western set from *Nope*, and a real 747 plane crash from the set of *War of the Worlds*. A fan favorite is seeing the famous clock tower from *Back to the Future*; however, this location is one of the most popular for filming, so make sure to book a multiday ticket for a chance to see it!

The Studio Tour operates all year, but since Universal is an active studio, there are times sets are unavailable due to production schedules. Make sure you set aside enough time during your day for this attraction. It takes approximately one hour to experience.

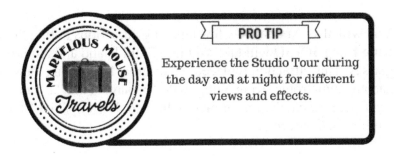

PRO TIP

Experience the Studio Tour during the day and at night for different views and effects.

If you are a big television and movie buff, you will want to book the VIP Tour. On a VIP Tour, you and your travel party will have your own tram and be able to actually walk through the sets! This is an incredibly immersive, one-of-a-kind experience, walking the same roads as many Hollywood legends!

During Halloween, the Studio Tour turns into the Terror Tram and is a part of Halloween Horror Nights! The Studio Tour will run as normal during regular park hours and become the Terror Tram during the Halloween Horror Nights event!

Whether looking for a fun experience for the whole family or a once-in-a lifetime memory, the world famous Studio Tour is one not to miss during your visit to Universal Studios Hollywood!

VIP TOURS

If you want to make the most of your visit to Universal Studios Hollywood or truly feel like a star, then you need to consider a VIP Tour! You will receive front-of-the-line access, see backstage areas, experience a private backlot tour, eat delicious (and included) food, and learn so much from your guide! It is the way to go to get the full Hollywood experience!

There are three different VIP tours to choose from year-round. Let's take a look and compare the three to see which one would work best for you!

VIP Tours

Universal Studios Hollywood

	VIP EXPERIENCE	PRIVATE VIP EXPERIENCE	PRIVATE VIP THEME PARK EXPERIENCE
Starting Price	$379/person		$2,299 for 4 $399 per additional person
Max Guests per tour	13	24	13
Tour Length	6.5-7 hours	6.5-7 hours	4-5 hours
Minimum Age	5	No mimimum age	No mimimum age
Meal Inclusions	Light Snacks & Refreshments in VIP Lounge. All you can eat gourmet meal in VIP dining area.	Light Snacks & Refreshments in VIP Lounge. All you can eat gourmet meal in VIP dining area.	Light Snacks & Refreshments in VIP Lounge. Choice of meal at either The Three Broomsticks in the Wizarding World of Harry Potter, or Krusty Burger in Springfield.
Valet Parking Included	Yes	Yes	Yes
Super Nintendo World	Enter at any time (even if vq reservations are required). VIP/Express Line access to Mario Kart: Bowser's Challenge (Before, during and after your tour)	Enter at any time (even if vq reservations are required). VIP/Express Line access to Mario Kart: Bowser's Challenge (Before, during and after your tour)	Enter at any time (even if vq reservations are required). VIP/Express Line access to Mario Kart: Bowser's Challenge (Before, during and after your tour)
Studio Backlot Tour	Private Backlot Tour, ability to walk around sets, visit to props department.	Private Backlot Tour, ability to walk around sets, visit to props department.	Not Included

All VIP Tours start in the VIP Lounge. You will enter through the VIP entrance located to the right of the general admission turnstiles and check-in for your tour. You can check-in early for your VIP Tour; this will give you access to your credentials to enter Super Nintendo World and use the VIP line for Mario Kart: Bowser's Challenge. Just make sure you leave enough time to get back to the lounge and enjoy some bites to eat before meeting your guide and starting your tour! There is also some cool memorabilia in the lounge, so make sure you take a good look around.

PRO TIP

Your park admission is included with your VIP Tour!

When you head out with your guide, you will learn about the history of the park, fun facts about rides/attractions, and skip ride lines, often including access to backstage areas! You will also receive priority seating for shows including WaterWorld. If you are on a VIP or Private VIP Tour, you will take a break halfway through for lunch at Moulin Rouge. This is the exclusive VIP dining area. It is a delicious all-you-can-eat buffet lunch, and you may even get to meet characters that occasionally roam through the restaurant! You can choose from inside dining or outside on the patio for a wonderful view. If you are doing the theme park VIP Tour, you will have your choice of a meal at either the Three Broomsticks or Krusty Burger.

One of the best parts of the VIP Tours (in our opinion) is the Studio Tour! You and your travel party will get your own tour tram! You will be able to pull over and explore some of the iconic and historic sets on the tour, take pictures, and learn all about the different shows and movies that have been filmed there. You will also get to visit the props department which is full of incredible props from major movies and television shows. Since it is a working studio, you may also spot some items that are tagged for use in things that are currently being filmed. You may also get to see some shows or movies being filmed! It is a truly amazing experience and well worth the cost of the tour for this portion alone! *NOTE: This is not included on the theme park only VIP Tour.*

If you are a Super Nintendo fan, this is another reason to consider adding a VIP Tour to your trip. During busier times of the year, Super Nintendo World may require a virtual queue to enter the land. But, if you are a VIP Tour guest, you can bypass that system entirely. You will be able to just show your lanyard and pass right by the long lines to get ready to race all day!

Ready to book your VIP Experience? Contact your Marvelous Mouse Travels agent to help you find the perfect VIP Tour experience for you!

> A VIP TOUR AT UNIVERSAL STUDIOS HOLLYWOOD IS A MUST! I LOVED BEING ABLE TO NOT ONLY WALK RIGHT INTO RIDES BUT ALSO GET TO SEE SO MUCH BEHIND THE SCENES! MY FAVORITE PART WAS THE PRIVATE STUDIO TOUR AND GETTING TO WALK AROUND DIFFERENT SETS AND EVEN TOUR THE PROPS DEPARTMENT! A VIP TOUR IS WORTH IT FOR THE STUDIO TOUR PORTION ALONE!
>
> -CHELSEA H

UNIVERSAL CITYWALK HOLLYWOOD

Universal CityWalk Hollywood is your one-stop destination for delicious food, shopping, entertainment, and nightlife outside of the theme park!

HOURS OF OPERATION

11:00 AM - 9:00 PM
Hours may vary.

DIRECTIONS TO CITYWALK

Address:
100 Universal City Plaza
Universal City, California 91608

For general directions to the Universal Studios Hollywood park, please see the options below:

From Hollywood

Take the 101 Hollywood Freeway North to Universal Studios Boulevard. Turn right onto Universal Studios Boulevard. Follow signs to Universal Studios Hollywood.

From Santa Monica

Take the 10 Santa Monica Freeway East to the 405 Freeway North. Exit to the 101 Ventura Freeway East/South. (Signs to Los Angeles) Continue on the 101 Freeway and exit on Lankershim Boulevard. Turn right on Lankershim Boulevard and follow the signs to Universal Studios Hollywood.

From the Los Angeles International Airport (LAX)

Follow signs to the 105 Freeway. Take the 105 Freeway East to the 110 Harbor Freeway North. After passing through the downtown area, get on the 101 Hollywood Freeway North. Follow the 101 Freeway to the Universal Studios Boulevard exit. Turn right on to Universal Studios Boulevard and follow the signs to Universal Studios Hollywood.

From Anaheim

Take the 5 Golden State Freeway North. Exit to the 101 Hollywood Freeway North. Continue on the 101 Freeway and exit at Universal Studios Boulevard. Turn right on to Universal Studios Boulevard and follow the signs to Universal Studios Hollywood.

From San Diego

Take the 5 Golden State Freeway North. Exit to the 101 Hollywood Freeway North. Continue on the 101 Freeway and exit at Universal Studios Boulevard. Turn right on to Universal Studios Boulevard and follow the signs to Universal Studios Hollywood.

From Santa Barbara

Take the 101 Hollywood Freeway South and exit on Lankershim Boulevard. Turn right on Lankershim Boulevard and follow the signs to Universal Studios Hollywood.

PARKING

Daily Parking Fees, Per Vehicle

General Parking before 5:00 PM - $32
General Parking after 5:00 PM - $10
Preferred Parking before 5:00 PM - $50
Preferred Parking after 5:00 PM - $20
Front Gate Parking - $70
General Parking is subject to availability. Parking rate may change without notice.

Valet Parking Standard Rates

$25 for First 2 Hours
$50 after 2 Hours

Valet Parking With Validation from CityWalk Full-Service Restaurant

Antojitos Cocina Mexicana
Bubba Gump Shrimp Co.
Buca di Beppo
Dongpo Kitchen
Jimmy Buffett's Margaritaville
Johnny Rockets
NBC Sports Grill & Brew
The Toothsome Chocolate Emporium & Savory Feast Kitchen
VIVO Italian Kitchen
Wasabi

$10 for 0 - 2.5 Hours
$15 for 2.5 - 3.5 Hours
$50 after 3.5 Hours

General Parking and a Movie Ticket

Enjoy $5 parking with purchase of General Parking and a movie ticket.

Offer is valid only at Universal Cinema at Universal CityWalk Hollywood. Offer is for one time use and must be surrendered at time of redemption. To receive your $5 parking, present your General Parking receipt at the Universal Cinema ticket window. Offer cannot be combined with any other promotional offers, discounts, or prior purchases. Offer subject to change without notice.

Electric Vehicle Charging Stations

Frankenstein Garage: 4 ports (Level 2 and Level 7)
Jurassic Parking Garage: 8 ports (Level 1 and B1M)
E.T. Garage: 16 ports (Level B1)
Woody Woodpecker Lot: 1 port (near Front Gate Parking)
Curious George Garage: 2 ports (Level 1)

Uber/Lyft

There are two rideshare locations at Universal Studios Hollywood-Level 7 of the Frankenstein Parking Lot, which is closer to the theme park entrance, or near Buca di Beppo, which is closer to CityWalk depending on how you want to start your day!

DINING

Full Service Dining Options

Antojitos Cocina Mexicana- Experience authentic Mexican cuisine, serving traditional dishes including guacamole and tacos. 100 + tequilas, handcrafted cocktails, and draft beers are also available.
- Open for lunch and dinner
- Advanced Reservations Available
- Price Range: $30 and under
- Fan Favorite: **Burria Tacos**
-

Bubba Gump Shrimp & Co- Immerse yourself in the beloved movie Forest Gump with southern home decor, memorabilia, photos, costumes, and, of course, all of the shrimp you can eat!
- Open for lunch and dinner
- Advanced Reservations Not Available
- Price Range: $38 and under
- Fan Favorite: **Shrimp Scampi**

Buca di Beppo- Feel like you are part of the family with delicious authentic Italian dishes including pasta, pizza, chicken parmesan, spaghetti and meatballs, and so much more!
- Open for lunch and dinner
- Advanced Reservations Available
- Food is served family-size
- Price Range: $33-$59 depending on portion size.
- Fan Favorite: **Chicken Parmesan**

Dongpo Kitchen- Experience the modernization and tradition of Sichuanese cuisine.
- Open for lunch and dinner
- Advanced Reservations Not Available

- Price Range: $30 and under
- Fan Favorite: **Dan Dan Noodles** and **Sichuan Dumplings**

Jimmy Buffett's Margaritaville- Relax and sip on a margarita while listening to the great hits of Jimmy Buffet! Enjoy island cuisine and what else? A Cheeseburger in Paradise!
- Open for lunch and dinner
- Advanced Reservations Available
- Price Range: $36 and under
- Fan Favorite: **Fish Tacos**

NBC Sports Grill & Brew- Catch the big game and enjoy favorites such as jalapeno poppers, wings, and burgers!
- Open for lunch and dinner
- Advanced Reservations Available
- Price Range: $30 and under
- Fan Favorite: **Grilled Cedar Plank Salmon**

The Toothsome Chocolate Emporium & Savory Feast Kitchen- Steaks, seafood, or brunch favorites… or skip right to the delicious desserts including over-the-top milkshakes!
- Open for brunch, lunch, and dinner.
- Advanced Reservations Available
- Price Range: $34 and under
- Fan Favorite: **Jacques' Specialty Flight-** Choose 5 Flavors: Brownie, Cookie Jar, Marshmallow Crisp, That's Mint, Thrilla in Vanilla, Red Velvet, Expresso Buzzzz, Heavenly Hazelnut, or Chocolate x5.

Vivo Italian Kitchen- Taste your way around Italy from homemade pasta and hand tossed pizzas to chicken piccata and fresh desserts.
- Open for lunch and dinner.
- Advanced Reservations Not Available
- Price Range: $34 and under
- Fan Favorite: **Quattro Formaggi Pizza**

Wasabi- Experience freshly made sushi and other innovative dishes!
- Open for lunch and dinner.
- Advanced Reservations Available
- Price Range: $28 and under
- Fan Favorite: **Salmon Sashimi**

Quick Service Dining and Snacks Options

Ben & Jerry's- Ice cream
Chick Chick Chicken- Chicken sandwiches and baskets
Cinnabon- Classic cinnamon roll and coffee
Firehouse Subs- Speciality or create-your-own subs
Jamba Juice- Smoothies
KFC Express/Pizza Hut Express- Favorite sandwiches, bowls, and pizza
Panda Express- Chinese food on-the-go
Pink's Famous Hot Dogs- Hotdogs and burgers
Taco Bell- Tacos, burritos, and nachos
The Crepe Café- Sweet and savory crepes, made fresh
The Habit Burger Grill- Made-to-order chargrilled burgers, sandwiches, and salads
Voodoo Doughnut- More than 50 kinds of fresh donuts
Starbucks- Coffees, teas, pastries, and sandwiches
Wetzels Pretzels- Hand-rolled pretzels
Johnny Rockets- Burgers, chicken sandwiches, milkshakes

SHOPPING

Abercrombie & Fitch- American Fashion Brand best known for preppy and trendy apparel
Billabong- One stop shop for your beach, snow and skate apparel, and accessories
Dodgers Clubhouse Store- Exclusive Dodgers apparel, accessories, and memorabilia
Hot Topic- Pop culture and music merchandise
Lids- Wide selection of hats and other accessories
Nectar Bath Treats- Plant-based soaps, scrubs, and bath bombs
Sephora- Makeup, skin care, and beauty supplies
Shoe Palace- The latest in athletic footwear
Sunsations- Largest collection of sunglasses

SUPER NINTENDO WORLD STORE on CityWalk- Wide selection of merchandise for all Nintendo Fans
The Los Angeles Sock Market- Socks for all occasions
The Raider Image- Exclusive Raiders merchandise, apparel, and memorabilia
Things From Another World- Collection of comics, collectibles, and graphic novels
Tillys- Skate, surf, and streetwear apparel and accessories
Universal Studios Store- Merchandise, toys, and gifts from your favorite movies and characters

All stores are open daily from 11:00 AM - 10:00 PM. Hours may vary.

ENTERTAINMENT

5 Towers Stage- State-of-the-art concert venue. Ticket availability and price depend on the event.

Access Hollywood- Seasonal event.

iFLY- Experience flight in an indoor skydiving wind tunnel! No experience necessary. Flight experiences available for ages three and older.
Pricing begins at $89 per person.
Discounts available for Annual Passholders.
Hours of Operation: Monday, and Saturday from 12:00 PM - 7:00 PM. Tuesday, Wednesday and Thursday from 9:00 AM - 4:00 PM. Friday and Sunday from 10:00 AM - 5:00 PM.

Universal Cinema- Catch the newest movies in these state-of-the-art theaters with deluxe power reclining seats.

So, whether you are looking to dine at one of the amazing restaurants, catch a movie, or shop for some of the newest Universal apparel, you can always find something to do in between your park time at Universal CityWalk Hollywood!

SHERATON UNIVERSAL HOTEL

Address:
>333 Universal Hollywood Drive
>Universal City, California 91608

Telephone: 818-980-1212

Check In Time: 4:00 PM
Check Out Time: 11:00 AM

WHAT MAKES THE SHERATON UNIVERSAL HOTEL MARVELOUS?

The Sheraton Universal Hotel is located within walking distance of both Universal Studios Hollywood and the Red Line Metro Station, making it perfect for those who want to visit Universal and explore LA. This hotel is a AAA 4-Diamond property that pays homage to the glitz and glamor of Old Hollywood while still offering sleek and modern decor and offerings.

HOTEL AMENITIES
- On-Site Restaurant
- Business Center
- Meeting Rooms
- EV Charging Station
- Fitness Center
- Events Venues
- Accessible Common Areas and Guest Rooms Available
- Outdoor Pool
- Pet-Friendly
- 24-Hour Room Service
- Complimentary WiFi
- Dry Cleaning Service
- Mobile Key/Digital Check In

STANDARD IN-ROOM AMENITIES
- Lighted Makeup Mirror
- Hair Dryer
- Alarm Clock
- In-Room Safe
- Cable/Satellite
- HBO
- Radio
- Mini Coolers
- Coffee Makers with Starbucks Coffee
- State of the Art Televisions

GUEST ROOM CATEGORIES

Guest Room Categories

Universal Studios Hollywood
Sheraton Universal Hotel

TYPE	CONNECTING ROOMS AVAILABLE	SQUARE FOOTAGE	HANDICAP ACCESSIBLE	MAXIMUM OCCUPANCY
Traditional Guest Room - King	Yes	325 sq ft	Yes	2
Traditional Guest Room - 2 Queens	Yes	325 sq ft	Yes	4
Traditional Guest Room - 2 Doubles	Yes	325 sq ft	No	4
Premium Lanai Guest Room - 2 Queens	Yes	350 sq ft	No	4
Family Guest Room - King Bed & sofa bed	Yes	325-350 sq ft	Hearing Accessible Only	4
Premium Corner Guest Room - 1 King & sofa bed	No	335 sq ft	No	4
Junior Suite - 1 King	No	525 sq ft	No	2
Suite - 2 Doubles & sofa bed	No	600 sq ft	No	6
Suite - 1 King & sofabed	Yes	600 sq ft	No	4
Executive Club Lounge Access - King	Yes	325 sq ft	No	2
VIP Suite	Yes	975 sq ft	No	3
Hospitality Suite	No	465 sq ft	No	4

CLUB LEVEL LOUNGE AMENITIES
- Open 24/7
- Private Access Floor
- Complimentary Food (Continental Breakfast, Midday Snacks, Hors D'oeuvres)
- Starbucks Coffee, Tea, and Espresso
- High-Speed WiFi
- Evening Bar Service

DINING
The California's- This is the hotel's signature restaurant, open every day for breakfast, lunch and dinner.

Terrace Bar- This bar is located poolside and open seasonally, serving a wide variety of cocktails and appetizers with a California-inspired flair.

In the Mix- Located right in the hotel lobby, this is the perfect spot to grab a drink or quick bite to eat.

24/7 Room Service

RECREATION
- Outdoor Pool
- Whirlpool
- Poolside Games
- Fitness Center

PARKING AND TRANSPORTATION
- Self Parking: $46.20 per day
- Valet Parking: $55 per day
- Short Walk to Universal Studios Hollywood
- Complimentary Shuttle to Universal Studios Hollywood
- Electric Car Charging Station (can be added for an additional $15 fee)
- Accessible Van Parking

HOTEL PET POLICY
- Non-Refundable Fee: $75
- Maximum Weight: 40 pounds
- 1 pet per guest allowed.
- A signed waiver is required at check-in.

HILTON LOS ANGELES/UNIVERSAL CITY

Address:
   555 Universal Hollywood Drive
   Universal City, California 91608
Telephone: 818-506-2500

Check In Time: 4:00 PM
Check Out Time: 11:00 AM

WHAT MAKES THE HILTON LOS ANGELES/UNIVERSAL CITY MARVELOUS?

The location of Hilton Los Angeles/Universal City makes it an exceptional choice for visitors. Situated just half a mile away from Universal Studios Hollywood, guests have convenient access to the theme park. Additionally, the hotel's proximity to the Red Line Metro Station further enhances accessibility, facilitating seamless exploration of the diverse attractions and landmarks scattered throughout the vibrant city of Los Angeles. This hotel is also pet-friendly and features a shuttle service to Universal Studios Hollywood.

HOTEL AMENITIES
- On-Site Restaurant
- Business Center
- Meeting Rooms
- EV Charging Station
- Fitness Center
- Outdoor Pool
- Pet-Friendly
- 24-Hour Room Service
- Complimentary WiFi

STANDARD IN-ROOM AMENITIES
- Scald-Proof Shower/Tub
- Coffee Maker
- 250-Thread Count Sheets
- 27" Television
- Air Conditioning
- Black-Out Curtains
- HBO
- Coffee Maker
- Hair Dryer
- Iron and Ironing Board
- Mini Fridge
- Bathroom Amenities
- Connecting Rooms
- Radio Alarm Clock

Guest Room Categories

Universal Studios Hollywood
Hilton Los Angeles / Universal City

TYPE	CONNECTING ROOMS AVAILABLE	SQUARE FOOTAGE	HANDICAP ACCESSIBLE	MAXIMUM OCCUPANCY
2 Double Beds	YES	118 Sq. Ft.	YES	4
2 Double Beds Executive Floor (with and without view of Universal Hollywood)	YES	118 Sq. Ft.	NO	4
1 King Bed	YES	115 Sq. Ft	YES	2
1 King Bed Executive Floor (with and without view of Universal Hollywood)	YES	115 Sq. Ft	NO	2
1 King Bed Corner Room with Sofa Bed (with and without view of Universal Hollywood)	YES	135 Sq. Ft	YES	4
1 King Bed Executive Floor Corner with Sofabed (with and without view of Universal Hollywood)	YES	135 Sq. Ft	NO	4
2 Queen Beds with and without view of Universal Hollywood)	YES	118 Sq. Ft	NO	4
2 Queen Beds 1 Bedroom Suite with Universal View	NO	246 Sq. Ft	NO	4
1 King Bed Directors Suite	NO	269 Sq. Ft.	NO	4
1 King Bed 1 Bedroom Suite	NO	259 Sq Ft.	NO	4
1 King Bed Diplomat Suite	NO	396 Sq. Ft.	NO	4

DINING

Atrium Lounge- Located in the hotel lounge, this is the perfect spot to grab a refreshing drink or tasty snack while listening to live music in the lobby.

Cafe Sierra- Enjoy a unique blend of California, Continental, and Chinese cuisine at this award-winning restaurant. They also offer an All-American breakfast buffet served daily, an Ultimate Seafood and Prime Rib Buffet served on Saturdays, and a Champagne Brunch served on Sundays.

Coffee Corner- Enjoy your favorite hot or cold coffee to kickstart your day.

Five on the Hill- Indulge in this elevated, outdoor dining experience with gorgeous views of Hollywood. The menu features fresh and locally-sourced ingredients. They also offer live music performances throughout the week.

Pool Bar and Grill- Enjoy your favorite drinks and tasty selections of burgers, sandwiches, and other options on the menu.

24/7 Room Service

RECREATION
- Outdoor Pool
- Whirlpool
- Fitness Center

PARKING AND TRANSPORTATION
- Self Parking: $45 + tax per night
- Valet Parking: $55 + tax per night
- Short walk to Universal Hollywood
- Complimentary Shuttle to Universal Studios Hollywood

HOTEL PET POLICY
- Non-Refundable Fee: $100
- Maximum Weight: 75 pounds
- 2 pets per guest allowed.
- Only domestic pets, such as cats and dogs, are allowed. Pets are not allowed unattended in the room.

THE GARLAND

Address:
    4222 Vineland Avenue
    North Hollywood, California 91602
Telephone: 818-766-0112

Check In Time: 3:00 PM
Check Out Time: 12:00 PM

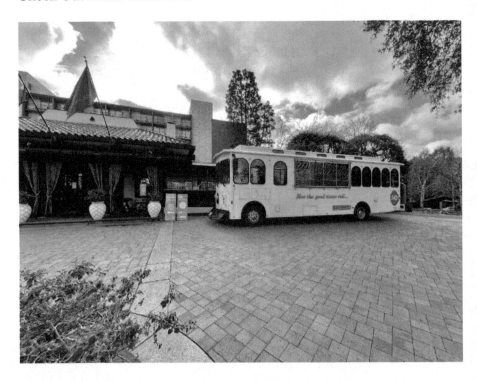

WHAT MAKES THE GARLAND MARVELOUS?

The Garland Hotel is an iconic North Hollywood hotel that was built by Fillmore Crank in 1970 for his wife Beverly Garland, a famous actress. This hotel offers the perfect combination of comfort, convenience, and hospitality for your visit to Universal Studios Hollywood. With its prime location, complimentary shuttle service, family-friendly accommodations, relaxing amenities, and warm hospitality, The Garland is perfect for most small and larger parties traveling to Universal Studios Hollywood! They are budget friendly and offer classic movies poolside on the big screen!

HOTEL AMENITIES

- 24-Hour Room Service
- Outdoor Pool and Hot Tub
- Trolley to Universal Studios Hollywood and Red Line Metro Station
- Fitness Center
- Pet-Friendly
- Laundry Facilities
- Complimentary WiFi
- Business Services
- Electric Car Charging Station
- Daily Buffet Breakfast (for a fee)

STANDARD IN-ROOM AMENITIES

- Private Balcony
- LED Flat Screen Televisions
- In-Room Entertainment System (Enseo)
- Refrigerator/Beverage Cooler
- In-Room Safe
- Pasadena-Based and Sustainable Bath Products
- Single Cup Coffee Brewer with Complimentary Coffee and Tea
- Hair Dryer
- Steam

Guest Room Categories

Universal Studios Hollywood
The Garland

TYPE	CONNECTING ROOMS AVAILABLE	SQUARE FOOTAGE	HANDICAP ACCESSIBLE	MAXIMUM OCCUPANCY
Deluxe King	YES	247 Sq. Ft	YES	3
Deluxe 2 Queen	YES	247 Sq. Ft.	YES	4
Premium King (with and without Pool View)	YES	331 Sq. Ft.	NO	3
Portola Suite	YES	560 Sq. Ft.	NO	4
Kids Room Suite	YES	331 Sq. Ft.	NO	4
Family Suite	YES	560 Sq. Ft	NO	5
The Carrington Suite	NO	675 Sq. Ft.	NO	6
The Filmore	NO	675 Sq. Ft.	NO	6
The Cathleen Suite	YES	675 Sq. Ft.	NO	6
Wellness Suite	NO	338 Sq Ft.	NO	2
The James Suite	NO	1006 Sq. Ft.	NO	2

DINING

The Front Yard- Offering a cozy and relaxed atmosphere, this restaurant is renowned for its diverse menu, blending comfort with culinary excellence. The Front Yard has something for every taste while providing a memorable experience of North Hollywood's vibrant culinary scene. The Front Yard is a well-known neighborhood gathering place that does an amazing job showcasing LA's diverse food culture, especially for brunch on the weekends.

The Lobby Bar- Grab a refreshing drink and delicious appetizers for a perfect way to end your day at the parks.

Taste of LA Taco Cart- Enjoy the hotel's poolside oasis in addition to their mouthwatering and flavorful Taco Cart.

RECREATION
- Outdoor Pool
- Fitness Center
- Movies by the Pool
- Yoga
- Foosball
- Seasonal Activities
- Bicycles (on request)
- Walking Distance to the Brady Bunch House

PARKING AND TRANSPORTATION
- Self Parking: $36 + tax per night
- Valet Parking: $39 + tax per night
- Complimentary Trolley to Universal Studios Hollywood and Los Angeles Red Line Metro Station (times subject to change at the discretion of The Garland)

The Garland Trolley Schedule

Universal Studios Hollywood / Universal City Walk / L.A. Metro Red Line Center

DEPART HOTEL	HOTEL RETURN
8:00 am	8:15 am
9:00 am	9:15 am
10:00 am	10:15 am
11;00 am	11:15 am
12:00 pm	12:15 pm
1:00 pm	1:15pm
2:00 pm	2:15pm
3:00 pm	3:15pm
4:00 pm	4:15 pm
5:00 pm	5:15 pm
6:00 pm	6:15 pm
7:00 pm	7:15pm
8:00 pm	8:15 pm
9:00 pm	9:15pm
10:00 pm	10:15pm

HOTEL PET POLICY

- Non-Refundable Fee: $75 (service animals are exempt from fee)
- Maximum Weight: 40 pounds
- 1 pet per guest allowed.
- All dogs will receive a dog toy, dog mat, and dog bowl with bottled water placed in the room during a client's stay. Dogs are not allowed unattended in the room.

SEASONAL EVENTS

The Garland is well known for their seasonal events including the Spring Block Party, live bands, and wine tastings. There is always something fun happening at this resort!

NEARBY HOTELS

TILT HOTEL UNIVERSAL/HOLLYWOOD
Address:
> 3241 Cahuenga Boulevard West
> Los Angeles, California 90068

Telephone: 213-319-7318
Distance to Universal Hollywood: 0.9 miles
Check In Time: 3:00 PM
Check Out Time: 12:00 PM
Minimum Check In Age: 21
Parking: $15 per day
Pet Policy: Pets Not Allowed
Key Hotel Amenities:
- Free High-Speed Wi-Fi
- Indoor Heated Pool
- Guest Laundry
- 24-Hour Front Desk
- Guest Copy Machine and Fax
- Self Indoor Parking

HOTEL AMARANO
Address:
> 322 North Pass Avenue
> Burbank, California 91505

Telephone: 818-842-8887
Distance to Universal Hollywood: 2.2 miles
Check In Time: 3:00 PM
Check Out Time: 11:00 AM
Minimum Check In Age: 21
Parking: Valet parking is included in property amenity fee.
Property Amenity Fee: $40 plus tax per day
Pet Policy: Two is the maximum number of pets allowed in a room.
> Pet fee per day, per pet is $150. Maximum pet weight is 50
> pounds.

Key Hotel Amenities:
- FYC Bar & Kitchen with Outdoor Dining
- Outdoor Heated Saltwater Pool
- Outdoor Hot Tub

76

- Complimentary Bike Rentals
- Fitness Center
- Poolside Daybeds
- 2,200 Square Feet of Event Space
- Event Catering
- Room Service
- Complimentary High-Speed WiFi

BEST WESTERN PLUS MEDIA CENTER INN & SUITES
Address:
> 3910 West Riverside Drive
> Burbank, California 91505

Telephone: 818-842-1900
Distance to Universal Hollywood: 2.3 miles
Check In Time: 3:00 PM
Check Out Time: 11:00 AM
Minimum Check In Age: 18
Parking: Complimentary parking
Pet Policy: Pets Not Allowed
Key Hotel Amenities:
- Complimentary Continental Breakfast
- Fitness Center
- Guest Laundry
- Safe Deposit Box
- Fax & Photocopy Services
- Ice/Vending Machines

LEXEN HOTEL NORTH HOLLYWOOD
Address:
> 5268 Tujunga Avenue
> North Hollywood, California 91601

Telephone: 828-821-3680
Distance to Universal Hollywood: 2.6 miles
Check In Time: 3:00 PM
Check Out Time: 11:00 AM
Minimum Check In Age: 21
Parking: $10 per night
Pet Policy: Pets Not Allowed
Key Hotel Amenities:

- Free High Speed WiFi
- Free Morning Coffee
- Fitness Room
- Meeting Room

LOEWS HOLLYWOOD HOTEL
Address:

1755 North Highland Avenue

Hollywood, California 90028

Telephone: 323-856-1200

Distance to Universal Hollywood: 3 miles

Check In Time: 4:00 PM

Check Out Time: 11:00 AM

Minimum Check In Age: 18

Parking: Public self-parking is $20 per night plus tax (does not include in-and-out privileges) and is available at Hollywood and Highland Center garages. Valet parking is $55 per night plus tax (includes in-and-out privileges).

Property Amenity Fee: $35 per day

Pet Policy: Two pets allowed per room. There is a charge of $100 per accommodation, per stay. Service animals are exempt from fees. All pets receive their own gifts including bowls and a special treat.

Key Hotel Amenities:
- Babysitting
- Business Center
- Concierge
- Conference Facilities
- Currency Exchange
- Dry Cleaning
- Fitness Center
- Free Wireless High-Speed Internet
- Safes and Safety Deposit Boxes
- Security
- Shoe Shine
- Rooftop Pool
- H2 Kitchen & Bar

HOLIDAY INN EXPRESS NORTH HOLLYWOOD
Address:
> 11350 Burbank Boulevard
> North Hollywood, California 91601

Telephone: 818-821-8031
Distance to Universal Hollywood: 3.4 miles
Check In Time: 3:00 PM
Check Out Time: 11:00 AM
Minimum Check In Age: 21
Parking: $15 per night
Pet Policy: Pets Not Allowed
Key Hotel Amenities:
- Full Hot Breakfast
- Outdoor Pool
- Fitness Center
- Guest Laundry Facilities
- Business Center
- WiFi Included

COAST ANABELLE HOTEL
Address:
> 2011 West Olive Avenue
> Burbank, California 91506

Telephone: 818-845-7800
Distance to Universal Hollywood: 3.7 miles
Check In Time: 4:00 PM
Check Out Time: 12:00 PM
Minimum Check In Age: 18
Parking: Complimentary parking
Shuttle Service: Complimentary, Monday through Sunday, 6:00 AM - 10:00 PM

Pet Policy: Pets Not Allowed
Key Hotel Amenities:
- Complimentary WiFi
- Business Services
- Concierge Desk
- Laundry/Valet Service
- Restaurant

- Room Service
- Tour/Sightseeing Desk
- Lounges/Bars

SAFARI INN, A COAST HOTEL
Address:
> 1911 West Olive Avenue
> Burbank, California 91506

Telephone: 818-845-8586
Distance to Universal Hollywood: 3.8 miles
Check In Time: 4:00 PM
Check Out Time: 12:00 PM
Minimum Check In Age: 18
Parking: Complimentary parking
Shuttle Service: Free Shuttle
Pet Policy: Two is the maximum number of pets allowed in a room.
> There is a $300 deposit required and $25 pet fee.

Key Hotel Amenities:
- Free WiFi
- Outdoor Swimming Pool
- Fitness Center
- Laundry Facilities
- Wake Up Service
- Vending Machines
- Luggage Storage
- Dry Cleaning
- Free Coffee (In-Room)

COMFORT INN & SUITES NEAR UNIVERSAL - N. HOLLYWOOD-BURBANK
Address:
> 6147 Lankershim Boulevard
> North Hollywood, California 91606

Telephone: 818-769-6600
Distance to Universal Hollywood: 4.4 miles
Check In Time: 3:00 PM
Check Out Time: 11:00 AM
Minimum Check In Age: 18
Parking: $19 per night

Pet Policy: Pets Not Allowed
Key Hotel Amenities:
- Free Hot Breakfast
- Premium Free WiFi
- Outdoor Pool
- Fax Machine
- Copy Machine
- Vending Machines

LOS ANGELES MARRIOTT BURBANK AIRPORT
Address:
>2500 North Hollywood Way
>Burbank, California 91505

Telephone: 818-843-6000
Distance to Universal Hollywood: 4.6 miles
Check In Time: 4:00 PM
Check Out Time: 12:00 PM
Minimum Check In Age: 21
Parking: Hourly: $6.72 / Daily $26.88 / Weekly: $188.16
Shuttle Service: There are two shuttles to Universal in the AM and two shuttles from Universal in the PM. Advanced reservations are required.
Pet Policy: Two is the maximum number of pets allowed in a room. Non-refundable pet fee per stay is $100. Maximum pet weight is 25 pounds.
Key Hotel Amenities:
- Outdoor Pool
- Whirlpool
- Fitness Center
- Airport Shuttle
- Beauty Shop
- Barber
- Meeting Event Space
- Cash Machine/ATM
- Concierge Desk
- Concierge Lounge Hours
- Cocktail Lounge With Light Fare
- Valet Same Day Dry Cleaning
- Coffee/Tea In Room

- Newspaper in Lobby
- Safe Deposit Boxes
- Laundry Facilities
- Vending Machines
- Room Service
- Gift/Newsstand

COURTYARD LOS ANGELES BURBANK AIRPORT

Address:

> 2100 Empire Avenue
> Burbank, California 91504

Telephone: 818-843-5500

Distance to Universal Hollywood: 5.2 miles

Check In Time: 4:00 PM

Check Out Time: 11:00 AM

Minimum Check In Age: 21

Parking: $22 per day

Pet Policy: Dogs are welcome. Two is the maximum number of pets allowed in a room. Non-refundable pet fee per stay is $150.

Key Hotel Amenities:

- Outdoor Pool
- Fitness Center
- Whirlpool
- Free WiFi
- Restaurant
- Meeting Space
- Convenience Store
- Gift Shop
- Dry Cleaning Service
- Laundry
- Wake Up Calls
- Mobile Key
- Digital Check In

HAMPTON INN & SUITES LOS ANGELES BURBANK AIRPORT

Address:

> 7501 North Glenoaks Boulevard
> Burbank, California 91504

Telephone: 818-768-1106
Distance to Universal Hollywood: 5.8 miles
Check In Time: 4:00 PM
Check Out Time: 11:00 AM
Minimum Check In Age: 18
Parking: Valet parking is $26 per night plus tax
Pet Policy: Dogs and cats are welcome. Two is the maximum number of pets allowed in a room. Non-refundable pet fee is $50 (1-4 night stay) and $75 (5+ night stay).
Key Hotel Amenities:
- Free Hot Breakfast
- Outdoor Pool
- Fitness Center
- Business Center
- Meeting Rooms
- Airport Shuttle
- Concierge
- EV Charging
- Free WiFi

RAMADA PLAZA BY WYNDHAM WEST HOLLYWOOD HOTEL & SUITES
Address:
    8585 Santa Monica Boulevard
    West Hollywood, California 90069
Telephone: 1-800-466-1589
Distance to Universal Hollywood: 6.1 miles
Check In Time: 3:00 PM
Check Out Time: 11:00 AM
Minimum Check In Age: 18
Parking: $55 per night
Pet Policy: Pets Not Allowed
Key Hotel Amenities:
- Free WiFi
- Outdoor Pool
- Fitness Center
- ATM
- Business Center
- Cafe

- Restaurant
- Laundry Services
- Dry Cleaning Services
- Guest Laundry
- Car Rental Desk
- Meeting Room
- EV Charging
- Sundries/Mart
- Safe Deposit Box

SPRINGHILL SUITES LOS ANGELES BURBANK-DOWNTOWN

Address:

549 South San Fernando Boulevard

Burbank, California 91502

Telephone: 818-524-2730

Distance to Universal Hollywood: 7.2 miles

Check In Time: 4:00 PM

Check Out Time: 12:00 PM

Minimum Check In Age: 18

Parking: $25 per day

Pet Policy: Two is the maximum number of pets allowed in a room. Non-refundable pet fee per stay is $150. Maximum pet weight is 50 pounds.

Key Hotel Amenities:
- Free WiFi
- Free Hot Breakfast
- Outdoor Pool
- Restaurant
- Fitness Center
- Convenience Store
- Laundry
- Dry Cleaning Service
- Wake Up Calls
- Digital Check In

HILTON GARDEN INN BURBANK DOWNTOWN
Address:

     401 South San Fernando Boulevard

     Burbank, California 91502

Telephone: 818-509-7964

Distance to Universal Hollywood: 7.2 miles

Check In Time: 3:00 PM

Check Out Time: 12:00 PM

Minimum Check In Age: 18

Parking: $22 per day

Pet Policy: Dogs and cats are welcome. Two is the maximum number of pets allowed in a room. Non-refundable pet fee is $50 (1-4 night stay) and $75 (5+ night stay).

Key Hotel Amenities:
- On-Site Restaurant
- Room Service
- Outdoor Pool
- Fitness Center
- Business Center
- Meeting Rooms
- EV Charging
- Free WiFi

RESIDENCE INN LOS ANGELES BURBANK-DOWNTOWN
Address:

     321 Ikea Way

     Burbank, California 91502

Telephone: 818-260-8787

Distance to Universal Hollywood: 7.7 miles

Check In Time: 4:00 PM

Check Out Time: 12:00 PM

Minimum Check In Age: 18

Parking: $22 per day

Pet Policy: Non-refundable pet fee per room is $150.

Key Hotel Amenities:
- Free WiFi
- Free Full American and Hot Breakfast
- Outdoor Pool
- Restaurant

- Meeting Space
- Gift Shop
- Fitness Center
- Laundry
- Dry Cleaning Service
- Wake Up Calls
- Digital Check In

BEST WESTERN PLUS CARRIAGE INN

Address:

5525 Sepulveda Boulevard

Sherman Oaks, California 91411

Telephone: 818-787-2300

Distance to Universal Hollywood: 7.5 miles

Check In Time: 3:00 PM

Check Out Time: 12:00 PM

Minimum Check In Age: 18

Parking: $12 per day

Shuttle Service: Available from 10:00 AM - 6:00 PM. Advanced reservations required.

Pet Policy: Two dogs are allowed and other pet types (i.e. cats) may be allowed upon the hotel's approval prior to arrival. Maximum pet weight is 80 pounds. Pet rate is $40 per day. A refundable cleaning and damage deposit of $150 is required upon check-in.

Key Hotel Amenities:
- Outdoor Pool
- Guest Laundry
- Dry Cleaning
- Restaurant
- Cocktail Lounge
- Fitness Center
- Car Rental Desk
- Safe Deposit Box

PHOTO OPPORTUNITIES AND CHARACTER MEET-AND-GREETS

There are plenty of opportunities to meet iconic characters from the past and the newest characters to the Universal family at Universal Studios Hollywood. Here, you will find characters that will appeal to every age group! Whether you would like to meet the famous Marilyn Monroe or interact with a Raptor, Universal Studios Hollywood has your character meet-and-greets covered. Character experiences at Universal Studios Hollywood are unique as each character really takes the time to meet you and pose for photo opportunities together!

The Upper Lot has a lot to offer for character experiences. From the moment you walk down the entrance/red carpet, you will start to see characters. Marilyn Monroe is available for a very chic and retro photo opportunity, while directly across from her, you will find Hello Kitty ready for her closeup. And, if you are lucky, you may spot Curious George walking around looking for his favorite snack! You will also want to keep your eyes peeled as you never know when Beetlejuice might pop up in the Upper Lot with his wild antics and mischievous grin!

A little bit further down the road, you will find Donkey in front of the Kung Fu Panda 4D experience. Donkey's meet-and-greet is a truly fun and hilarious experience! But fair warning, if you wear any Disney merchandise, he will roast you! It is in this area that you will also find meet-and-greets with Shrek and Princess Fiona as well as your favorite stars from the Trolls movies. Branch, Poppy, and Guy Diamond all make a very colorful and fun appearance.

Heading down New York Street, you will run into the whole Scooby Doo gang and their mystery van, "The Mystery Machine." This is a great photo opportunity with a lot of characters! Around the same area, you can easily find Frankenstein and his Bride. Frankenstein has a limited vocabulary but is a great character for a freaky photo! And, Great Scott! You may even run into Doc from Back to the Future if you are fast enough to catch him. He is always in a rush trying to find the next invention. Also, keep your eyes peeled for straight-talking New Yorkers hanging out of the apartment windows. They have the gift of gab and will call out to you!

Don't forget to head over to Despicable Me: Minion Mayhem and Super Silly Fun Land. Here, you can meet Gru, the girls, and the Minions! This photo opportunity is a favorite and worth waiting for! If you are a fan of the Simpsons, make sure you also head to Springfield USA where you can meet characters like Bart, Lisa, Homer, and Marge!

Last, but not least, you must head over to Hogsmeade in The Wizarding World of Harry Potter. Here, you can meet the conductor of the Hogwarts Express. He is usually in a jolly mood and has some good tips.

Now, it is time to cruise on down to the Lower Lot. When you get to the bottom of the escalators, you will notice some prehistoric creatures directly to your left. Here is where you can find the Raptor Encounter with the new Triceratops. What is your guess on how many people are inside operating the Triceratops? It's a mystery, and we need to get to the bottom of it!

Are you an Autobots or Decepticon fan? One of the most unique character experiences is meeting with a transformer. They are larger than life and ready for a fun photo with you... Well, most of them... Here, you can meet and talk with Optimus Prime, Megatron, or Bumblebee. Even though the transformers will tower over you, they will take their time getting to know fun facts about you and even take selfies if you ask!

Power up in 3...2...1! It is time to step inside the Mushroom Kingdom and head into Super Nintendo World. Before you walk through Princess Peach's castle, you will have a fun photo opportunity in front. Sink in or pop out of the classic flowerpots from the original Super Mario Brothers' video game. Once you step inside, make sure to be on the lookout for Mario and Luigi. They are always a team and travel together. They also say their signature lines so listen closely! Toadstool will also come out and Princess Peach will make a grand entrance, as most princesses will do!

No matter where you are inside Universal Studios Hollywood, there are always characters roaming around and available to make your visit to this destination even more memorable... and you will have the photos to remember these moments forever!

THINGS TO DO AROUND UNIVERSAL STUDIOS HOLLYWOOD

Planning to visit Universal Studios Hollywood on your next vacation? Los Angeles is the perfect destination to add fun, sightsee, enjoy delicious food, and tour some of your favorite television show filming locations. Want to add some great experiences to your Universal Studios Hollywood vacation package? Be sure to reach out to your Marvelous Mouse Travels' agent for more information!

THINGS TO SEE AND DO AROUND LOS ANGELES

Tours

Warner Brothers Studio Tour: Explore the Backlot and experience over 100 years of movie-making history. Walk in the footsteps of some of your favorite actors and actresses.

Paramount Studio Tour: Take a 2-hour tour where you'll discover Hollywood's first major movie studio and visit locations like Bronson Gate, New York Street Backlot, and the Prop Warehouse.

TCL Chinese Theater Tour: This is the only tour in Hollywood that takes you inside the historic theater.

Dolby Theatre Tour: This tour offers a 30-minute guided tour which includes a visit to the theater, and VIP room, as well as learning about Oscar history.

Hollywood Movie Star Homes Tour: This top-rated Celebrity Stars home tour takes you to multiple tour stops and points of interest including celebrity homes.

Hollywood Behind the Scenes Tour: Learn about less well-known theaters and landmarks on this one-hour walking tour. You'll be escorted to some of Hollywood's famous landmarks as well.

Self-Guided Movie Star Homes Bike Tour: Receive a digital map and take a self-guided self-paced bike tour through Hollywood and Los Angeles.

Hollywood / Beverly Hills

Los Angeles Zoo and Botanical Gardens: The Los Angeles Zoo and Botanical Gardens is a 133-acre zoo located in Los Angeles. Find Chimpanzees of the Mahale Mountains, the Campo Gorilla Reservice, Elephants of Asia, and more.

Hollywood Hills Hike: Discover the best hiking paths around the Hollywood Sign including Mt. Hollywood Trail, Brush Canyon Trail, and Cahuenga Peak Trail.

Horseback Ride to the Hollywood Sign: Sightsee on horseback and get unforgettable views of the LA Basin and Hollywood Sign.

Griffith Park Observatory: The Observatory houses a planetarium and astronomy museum

Madame Tussauds Hollywood: Meet your favorite celebrities… in wax form!

Hollywood Walk of Fame: Be sure to check the Star Map to find your favorite stars located on the sidewalks along 15 blocks of Hollywood Boulevard.

Rodeo Drive: The iconic fashion street in Beverly Hills.

Hollywood Bowl Events: The best destination for concerts, shows, and events.

Museums

Getty Museum: The museum is home to European paintings, drawings, sculptures, manuscripts, art, and photography.
Hollywood Museum: This museum is the official museum of Hollywood with the most extensive collection of Hollywood memorabilia in the world.
Museum of Neon Art: Come experience neon, electric, and kinetic art.
Museum of Jurassic Technology: Learn all about artistic, scientific, and historic items
Los Angeles County Museum of Art (LACMA): This museum is the largest art museum in the western United States.
Museum of Illusions: This museum is a 3D Illusion and Upside-Down House exhibit where you'll get to experience all types of interactive interactions.
California Science Center: Experience multiple hands-on galleries, special exhibitions, IMAX movies, and more.

Theaters

Pantages Theatre: See your favorite Broadway performances take place here.
El Capitan Movie Theatre: This theater hosts movie premiers and other movie showings.
Live Audience Experiences: Want to be part of a live audience? Get your tickets here! https://1iota.com/

SPORTING EVENTS

Watch your favorite sports team during your next vacation to Los Angeles (depending on the season):
Football: LA Rams
Basketball: Lakers and Clippers
Baseball: Dodgers and Angels
Hockey: Kings and Ducks
Soccer: Los Angeles Galaxy (MLS) and Los Angeles FC (MLS)

SPLIT STAY WITH DISNEYLAND

Disneyland is about an hour from Universal Studios Hollywood, so it is easy to split your time between Universal Studios Hollywood and Disneyland! Experience the best of both destinations with a split-stay vacation option! Reach out to your Marvelous Mouse Travels' agent for more information regarding hotel and ticket packages; they will put together the perfect vacation to maximize your time at both locations!
Disneyland Park
Disney California Adventure Park
Attend a Special After-Hours Event like Oogie Boogie Bash

DINING OPTIONS OUTSIDE OF THE PARK

Universal CityWalk

CityWalk Hollywood Bubba Gump
Ca' Del Sole
Smoke House Restaurant
Porto's Bakery and Café

FIVE on the Hill
Bucca di Beppo
The Front Yard
Verse
In-N-Out Burger
Mercado
Vivian's Millennium Café
Bob's Big Boy
Miceli's

Hollywood

Musso and Frank
TAO Asian Bistro
In-N-Out Burger
Sweet Lily Bakery Café
Mercado

5 LA HOT SPOTS FOR THE BRAVO FANS

SUR Restaurant: Famous for the Bravo hit show "Vanderpump Rules"

TomTom: Named after Tom Schwartz and Tom Sandoval from Bravo's "Vanderpump Rules"

Schwartz and Sandy's: Tom Schwartz and Tom Sandoval's own bar from Bravo's "Vanderpump Rules"

Something About Her: Ariana Madix and Katie Maloney's own sandwich shop from Bravo's "Vanderpump Rules"

Jax's Studio City: Jax Taylor and Brittany Cartwright's own bar from Bravo's "Vanderpump Rules" and "The Valley."

BEST BEACHES

Santa Barbara
Malibu
Zuma Beach
Santa Monica Beach and Pier
Venice Beach
Laguna Beach
Santa Catalina Island

SEASONAL EVENTS AT UNIVERSAL STUDIOS HOLLYWOOD

Throughout the year, Universal Studios Hollywood dazzles guests with special events and celebrations that make every visit unforgettable. From spine-tingling Halloween Horror Nights to electrifying special events and fireworks displays, there is always a reason to celebrate at Universal Studios Hollywood. From the joyous festivities of the holiday season to the thrilling events that ignite the summer nights, there is always something extraordinary happening here. Universal Studio Hollywood hosts a variety of celebrations that capture the imagination and spirit of guests of all ages.

LUNAR NEW YEAR
Lunar New Year at Universal Studios Hollywood is an annual event held on select days in January and February. As you step into the park, you will be greeted by colorful décor and festive atmospheres that capture the spirit of the Lunar New Year. This event brings the rich traditions and cultural festivities of the Lunar New Year to life in the heart of Hollywood and generally features a wide variety of themed food, beverages, and merchandise. Snap photos and meet characters throughout the parks in special Lunar New Year attire. Typically, on

the weekends, the park hosts cultural performances. This is an amazing event that is only offered at Universal Studios Hollywood.

GRAD BASH

Get ready to celebrate your graduation in style at Universal Studios Hollywood's Grad Bash Night. This exclusive after-hours event, held on select nights in May and June, promises an unforgettable night of fun, excitement, and memories that will last a lifetime. With exclusive park access just for graduating seniors, students can enjoy their favorite rides and attractions with significantly shorter lines. It is the perfect way to experience the thrills of the park without the usual wait times. Dance the night away at multiple dance parties hosted by live DJs with each party area featuring its own unique vibe. Capture the magic of the night with special graduation-themed photo opportunities scattered throughout the park. From iconic Universal Studios landmarks to unique backdrops designed just for Grad Bash, these photos provide the perfect way to commemorate this milestone moment.

INDEPENDENCE DAY

Don't miss Universal Studios Hollywood's star-spangled Fourth of July celebration! Head to the park early for award-winning rides and attractions during the day. As you explore the park, you will be immersed in festive décor, setting the perfect patriotic backdrop for your day. From the adrenaline-pumping adventures of the Transformers ride to the magical world of Harry Potter, there is something for everyone to enjoy. As the day winds down, the excitement ramps up with the grand finale, fireworks! The show is synchronized to a mix of familiar Universal-themed music and patriotic favorites, creating a magical and awe-inspiring experience that will leave you in amazement. The best part? All the Fourth of July festivities are included in the price of your theme park admission! That means you can enjoy everything Universal Studios Hollywood has to offer, plus the special Independence Day celebrations, without any extra cost!

HALLOWEEN HORROR NIGHTS

Halloween Horror Nights is recognized as the scariest event in California; this spine-tingling celebration transforms the iconic theme park into a nightmarish realm where the most terrifying scenes from horror films and television shows come to life! The event typically runs from mid-September through early November, giving guests ample opportunity to partake in the festivities. Whether you're a seasoned horror fan or a newcomer to the world of fright, here is everything you need to know about experiencing Halloween Horror Nights Hollywood.

At the heart of Halloween Horror Nights Hollywood is its elaborately themed scarehouses, Terror Tram, and scare zones.

Scarehouses
Since 1986, Halloween Horror Nights Hollywood has featured eight scarehouses meticulously designed to immerse guests in the world of a specific horror story, complete with detailed sets, special effects, and costumed actors. These mazes are more than just haunted houses; they arc interactive experiences where guests can walk through scenes and encounter the creatures that inhabit them. Past houses have included themes such as Carnival of Carnage, The Walking Dead, The Last of Us, Halloween and so many more frightful experiences.

Terror Tram
Unique to Halloween Horror Nights Hollywood is the Terror Tram. The Terror Tram offers a terrifying journey through the iconic Universal backlot, where some of Hollywood's most famous horror movies were filmed. Each year, the Terror Tram features a new theme, often based on popular horror franchises or original concepts created by Universal's talented team of designers. Previous themes have included encounters with iconic horror villains like Jason Voorhees, Freddy Krueger, and the terrifying world of "The Purge." As you disembark from the tram and step into the darkness, you'll find yourself walking through detailed sets and encountering scareactors who are ready to bring your worst nightmares to life. Unlike traditional mazes, the Terror Tram allows you to explore larger outdoor areas, making the experience feel more real and unpredictable. If you book the RIP Tour, you will have an additional haunted house along the Terror Tram route. What a terrifying treat!

Scareactors
Now unlike Halloween Horror Nights Orlando, Halloween Horror Nights Hollywood does not have opening scaremonies, *however*, that does not mean you are safe from chainsaws and other terrifying scareactors. Periodically throughout the event, scareactors will stalk their prey. The interaction between scareactors and guests is what makes Halloween Horror Nights truly unique. Each scareactor's goal is to immerse guests in a world of horror, making them feel like they are part of a real-life nightmare.

Scarezones

In addition to the scarehouses, Halloween Horror Nights Hollywood also features three scarezones every season, where monsters, ghouls, and maniacs roam freely, ready to pounce on unsuspecting visitors. These zones are strategically placed throughout the park, ensuring that the fear factor is constant as guests move from one attraction to another. Scarezones are open areas within the park where scareactors freely roam. These zones are designed to keep guests on edge as they move between attractions. The scareactors here might be more interactive, engaging in short, terrifying encounters that leave a lasting impression.

Live Entertainment

Just when you thought there was nothing else that Universal Studios Hollywood could add to scare you, how can we forget about the live shows! In the past Universal Studios Hollywood has featured live performances by the award-winning hip hop crew, The Jabbawockeez. In 2023, they introduced a brand new live action show called "The Purge: Dangerous Waters," which offers a uniquely terrifying experience that blends the chaotic horror of *The Purge* with the eerie, unpredictable nature of water-based attractions. The attraction features highly skilled scareactors who bring the world of *The Purge* to life.

Another show that Halloween Horror Nights Hollywood introduced in 2023 was Blumhouse: Behind the Screams. This exhibit takes you on a journey through some of the creepiest movies released by Blumhouse including the highly anticipated films *Five Nights at Freddy's* and *The Exorcist: Believer*, as well as the fan-loving hits like *M3GAN* and *The Black Phone*. There were also photo opportunities with scareactors such as The Grabber from The Black Phone for only the bravest of park guests.

PRO TIP

Keep an eye out for the Death Eaters as they roam Hogsmeade, looking to challenge anyone who will not show loyalty to Voldemort's cause.

Specialty Food and Beverages

Something Universal Studios does an amazing job with is crafting a food and beverage menu that aligns with the various scarezones and scarehouses being featured each year. A newly themed refreshment area to Halloween Horror Nights in 2023 was The Peacock Halloween Horror Bar! Located near the WaterWorld Stage at the Laemmle Courtyard, this bar features some spooktacular-themed beverages including the Purge Punch as well as photo opportunities with the Bride of Frankenstein and David S. Pumpkin. This is a great spot to grab a drink before catching the show.

Another favorite spot, especially if you love Mexican food, is the La Plaza De Los Muertos. The entire plaza is adorned with traditional Día de los Muertos decorations, featuring skeleton figures, sugar skulls, papel picado (tissue paper flags), and vibrant flowers. As the sun sets and darkness falls upon the park, you will want to keep a watchful eye for scareactors that will float through the plaza including The Grey Lady. If you are a fan of margaritas, this is a great spot to try one of their delicious margaritas and other latin-inspired cocktails.

Merchandise

Now as you may or may not know, no Universal Studios event is complete without merch, so, whatever you do, do not leave your wallet at home! Regardless of the time of day, you can find a wide variety of Halloween Horror Nights-themed merchandise throughout the park and CityWalk! Everything from t-shirts, hoodies, tumblers, lanyards, backpacks, hats, and more is available for purchase! Halloween Horror Nights will start releasing its merchandise slowly about 3-4 months prior to the event starting. Once the event is in full swing, everything will be released into the stores and inventory does go fast. If you see something you really want in your size or style, do not hesitate in making that purchase.

Open Attractions

Now, sometimes we all need a break from the screaming and what better way than to enjoy some of the rides that are open during Halloween Horror Nights. Included in your event admission ticket is the ability to go on any of the open attractions. The attractions that are typically open during the event are:

- o Transformers
- o Revenge of the Mummy
- o Jurassic World
- o The Simpsons Ride
- o The Wizarding World with Death Eaters and Castle Projections
- o Harry Potter and the Forbidden Journey
- o Flight of the Hippogriff

There is one very important exception. There are only certain ticket types that can access Super Nintendo World during Halloween Horror Nights. The first one is the "Halloween Horror Nights After 2pm Day/Night" ticket which includes admission to Super Nintendo World only from 7:00 PM - 10:00 PM and may be subject to the Virtual Line depending on park capacity. This ticket also includes Early Event Access to select houses at 5:30 PM. The other ticket is the "Halloween Horror Nights After 2pm Day/Night Universal Express" ticket, which also includes admission to Super Nintendo World from 7:00 PM - 10:00 PM as well as Early Event Access to select houses starting at 5:30 PM. This ticket does not include Express access to Mario Kart: Bowser's Challenge.

Ticket Pricing (*rates based on 2023 pricing*)

Excited about Halloween Horror Nights? Let's talk about how you too can enjoy a night of fright and scares. Halloween Horror Nights Hollywood is a special event, so there is a separate ticket required for this event.

- • Halloween Horror Nights General Admission ticket pricing starts at $74 per person and does not include Early Event Access or Super Nintendo World access, however, that can be purchased separately.

103

- Halloween Horror Nights Universal Express Passes start at $209 per person and includes one-time express access to each participating scarehouse, open rides (Mario Kart is excluded), and attractions. Early Event Access and Super Nintendo World are not included.
- Halloween Horror Nights Universal Express Passes Unlimited start at $249 per person and includes unlimited express access to each participating scarehouse, open rides (Mario Kart is excluded), and attractions. Early Event Access and Super Nintendo World are not included.
- Halloween Horror Nights After 2pm Day/Night Ticket starts at $149 per person and includes admission to the theme park starting at 2:00 PM as well as same day evening admission to Halloween Horror Nights. This ticket also includes admission to Super Nintendo World from 7:00 PM - 10:00 PM and Early Event Access to the scarehouses starting at 5:30 PM.
- Halloween Horror Nights After 2pm Day/Night Universal Express Ticket starts at $329 per person and includes admission to the theme park starting at 2:00 PM, same day evening admission to Halloween Horror Nights, and one-time express line access to each ride, show and scarehouse. This ticket also includes admission to Super Nintendo World from 7:00 PM - 10:00 PM and Early Event Access to the scarehouses starting at 5:30 PM.
- Early Event Access Ticket starts at $10 per person and is a new add-on to any Halloween Horror Nights ticket; they are limited and do sell out. Early Access Tickets can access select houses 90-minutes prior to guests arriving at 7:00 PM. You must have an admission ticket for Halloween Horror Nights.

Frequent Fear Passes

If you are someone that loves Halloween and all things creepy then you will want to consider a Frequent Fear Pass, especially if you plan to visit Halloween Horror Nights multiple times in the season. A Frequent Fear Pass at Halloween Horror Nights is a special ticket option that allows guests to visit Universal Studios Hollywood's Halloween Horror Nights 30 times throughout the event season. This pass is designed for die-hard horror fans who want to experience the scares and thrills on multiple nights without purchasing a separate ticket each time. There are some blackout dates with this pass. The cost of this pass starts at $209 per person.

Another option with unlimited access to Halloween Horror Nights Hollywood is the Ultimate Fear Pass. The Halloween Horror Nights Ultimate Fear Pass is the top tier ticket option for Universal Studios Hollywood's Halloween Horror Nights. This pass is designed for the ultimate horror fan who wants unlimited access to the event throughout the entire season. This pass has no blackout dates and gives passholder access to ALL nights. The cost of this pass is $329 per person.

R.I.P Tour
The R.I.P. Tour at Universal Studios Hollywood's Halloween Horror Nights is the ultimate way to experience the event in style and comfort. Perfect for horror enthusiasts who want to make the most of their visit, the R.I.P. Tour combines priority access, exclusive perks, and luxury services to create an unforgettable night of terror and thrills. There are two different types of R.I.P Tours which are non-private and private that can accommodate up to 12 people per tour. A Private R.I.P Tour will only include members of your group whereas a Non-Private R.I.P Tour will have mixed parties. The perks to an R.I.P tour include:

- Admission to Halloween Horror Nights (no daytime admission or Early Event Access)
- Guided walking tour of the event
- One-time R.I.P. entry into each house as well as select rides and attractions while on tour with a guide
- Reserved seating at a live show while on tour with R.I.P. guide
- Express UNLIMITED access for the day of the tour on select rides, houses, and attractions
- Complimentary valet parking for one vehicle
- Special VIP entrance to Universal Studios Hollywood, commemorative R.I.P. credentials and lanyard
- Exclusive Universal Backlot Halloween experience with private VIP trolley transportation

- Gourmet dinner (alcoholic beverages excluded) in the private VIP dining room
- Access to cash bar locations available during the tour (must be 21 years old or older to purchase and consume alcoholic beverages with a valid photo ID)
- Access to an exclusive VIP house along the Terror Tram route

Tours usually start at 7:00 PM. Guests are strongly encouraged to arrive 30 minutes prior to the start of the tour. Tipping your R.I.P Tour Guide is strongly recommended!

Halloween Horror Nights Hollywood Event Plan

Halloween Horror Nights at Universal Studios Hollywood is an immensely popular event! In order to make the most of your visit and minimize wait times, it is essential to have a good plan in place. Here is a comprehensive strategy to help you navigate HHN efficiently:

- If you have access to early entry, take advantage of it to get a head start on the scarehouses. Early entry typically allows you to enter the park up to an hour before the official start time. This will also minimize your wait on some of the houses.
- Start with the scarehouses located at the Lower Lot. These tend to be less crowded at the beginning of the night. Most people start at the Upper Lot, so the scarehouses at the Lower Lot will have less wait times.
- Save the scarezones and the Terror Tram for when it is dark. This will intensify the experience.
- Plan to watch live shows mid-evening. This allows you to rest and recharge before tackling the Terror Tram or Scarehouses.
- The last hour of the event is often less crowded, providing an opportunity to experience popular scarehouses (perhaps for a second time) with shorter wait times.

Best Halloween Horror Nights Tips

- Friday and Saturday nights, especially the closer you get to Halloween, will be busier than other days (as well as opening weekend). If you would prefer not to deal with the crowds, it is strongly encouraged to consider alternate days.
- Do not wait to book your ticket or any special add-ons and express passes, as they will sell out, especially on peak nights

including Halloween! Pricing does also increase based on demand.

- Wear good footwear, such as sneakers, when headed to the parks. Universal Studios Hollywood was built on a hillside, and you will be doing a lot of walking. On the Terror Tram, you will be walking up and down hills.
- Eat a decent meal before the event (perhaps at CityWalk), so you are not wasting time during the event.
- If you do not have an Express Pass, start your night at Halloween Horror Nights Hollywood in the Backlot.
- Try not to use your Express Pass when you get to the park (unless you have Unlimited Express). Since you can only use the Express Pass one time per house, it is better to use it when the wait times are higher.
- Consider if this event is right for you and your family in advance. This event is mature in content, contains alcohol, and can have graphic language in shows. This event is not recommended for children under the age of 13.
- Remember, scareactors cannot touch you! But, if you touch them, you will be banned from the park. Universal takes the safety of their scareactors very seriously, and you do not want to jeopardize your time in the parks.

A Chicken's Guide to Surviving Halloween Horror Nights Hollywood
- Do your research about the scarehouses, scarezones, and live entertainment, so you know what to expect when you get to the park.
- Do not be afraid to take breaks or enjoy some rides to break up the scares. You may love all things Halloween, but the scares can be intense to some people.
- Grab your scream squad. Halloween Horror Nights is so much better with family and friends. Plus, having people you trust around will help you find the courage to conquer the houses!
- Go second to last in your group. Guests walk through the houses in a single file line. You do not want to be the last person, in case a scareactor is following you, and being the first person means you will experience the jump scares before anyone else in the line!

- Purchase an Express Pass. The longer you have to wait in line for a scarehouse, the more anxious you will become about the experience. Utilizing an Express Pass will cut your wait times down tremendously, lowering your anxiety.
- If you have sensitivity to loud noises, it is strongly recommended to purchase ear plugs. The scarehouses and scarezones do get loud and can overstimulate some people.
- Be on the lookout for scareactors. You never know where they will come from, and they love to catch people by surprise!
- Some houses are not for everyone, and that is ok! Do not be afraid to speak up and tell your scream squad if you need to skip a house. Only experience the scarehouses you are most comfortable with to ensure a memorable experience!

Halloween Horror Nights Hollywood VS Halloween Horror Nights Orlando

Halloween Horror Nights is a premier Halloween event held at both Universal Studios Hollywood and Universal Studios Florida. While both events share similarities in providing top-notch horror entertainment, there are distinct differences between the two that make each unique. Halloween Horror Nights Hollywood is slightly smaller but still packed with intense scares and high-quality mazes. Hollywood usually features around 7-8 haunted houses and fewer scarezones compared to Orlando. One of Hollywood's unique features is the Terror Tram, a backlot tour that transforms into a horrifying experience where guests walk through iconic movie sets turned into nightmarish scenes. Historically, the live entertainment is also different at Universal Studios Florida and Universal Studios Hollywood. There is also not an opening scaremony at Universal Studios Hollywood due to the layout of the park. But that does not mean they are lacking in scareactors, especially given their close ties and proximity to the film industry.

Universal Horror Unleashed!

Who says Halloween only has to happen in the fall? What if you could experience Halloween Horror Nights year round? Well, coming soon to Las Vegas, you can! Welcome Universal Horror Unleashed! The upcoming experiential attraction will be situated in Las Vegas as a component of AREA15, an immersive entertainment district. The 20-

acre space will showcase a range of distinctive, immersive, and horror-themed experiences, accompanied by spooky dining options and chilling bar areas. Unlike the annual Halloween Horror Nights scarehouses and scarezones, Universal Horror Unleashed will stand out by offering a continuously evolving experience with seasonal events and exclusive merchandise offerings. Although specific details about the venue's main attractions and opening date have not yet been revealed, guests can anticipate encountering a wide array of modern and classic horror icons from Universal's extensive repertoire, spanning from Universal Monsters to recent successes like *Chucky, The Purge, Nope,* and many more blood-curdling films!

In addition to Halloween Horror Nights in Universal Studios Hollywood, guests can also enjoy Halloween Horror Nights in Japan, Singapore, and Orlando, Florida.

THE HOLIDAYS

Spending the holidays at Universal Studios Hollywood is a festive way to enjoy the park! From the moment you enter, you will be immersed in the holiday spirit as Universal Studios Hollywood is adorned with dazzling lights, colorful ornaments, and festive decorations. Typically this event runs from early November through December, and most activities are included with admission. However, there are some add-ons that are an additional cost. Let's talk about all of the magical things guests can expect to experience when they spend the holidays at Universal Studios Hollywood.

Character Encounters
During the holiday season at Universal Studios Hollywood, guests can enjoy special character encounters that add an extra touch of magic and festivity to their visit. Throughout the park, guests will find

numerous photo opportunities with holiday-themed backdrops and decorations. Many characters, such as the Minions, Shrek, and Transformers will also adorn festive holiday attire. These characters will be scattered throughout the park, so make sure to have your cameras ready to grab some iconic photos. The photo opportunities available are perfect for capturing memories for holiday cards to share with family and friends.

Holiday-Themed Food and Beverages

During the holidays, Universal Studios Hollywood offers a delightful array of festive food and drinks that are sure to tantalize guests' taste buds. From traditional seasonal treats to unique culinary creations, there is something for everyone to enjoy. Quench your thirst with festive beverages that are perfect for sipping while strolling through the park. Enjoy classic holiday favorites like hot cocoa and specialty drinks such as Grinch's Heart, Fiesta Fizz, and more! Take a break from the excitement of the attractions and refuel with seasonal meals and snacks that are both delicious and satisfying! Some of these holiday options include holiday popcorn, chicken and waffles, snow globe cookies, clam chowder in a bread bowl, and more.

Holiday Merchandise

As with any special event at Universal Studios Hollywood, guests must purchase some exclusive, holiday-themed merchandise to commemorate their visit to Universal Studios Hollywood. From collectible ornaments and festive apparel to themed souvenirs and keepsakes, there is a wide array of holiday merchandise available throughout the park.

Christmas in The Wizarding World of Harry Potter
Experience the magic of the holiday season like never before inside
The Wizarding World of Harry Potter at Universal Studios
Hollywood! Step into the enchanting village of Hogsmeade, where
snow-capped rooftops and twinkling lights create a whimsical winter
wonderland. As guests stroll through the streets, they are immersed in
the sights, sounds, and smells of the wizarding world, decked out in
festive decorations inspired by the beloved Harry Potter series.

The Magic of Christmas at Hogwarts Castle
As dusk hits the Wizarding World, Hogwarts Castle will be adorned
with dazzling lights and projections that illuminate the night sky
during the "The Magic of Christmas at Hogwarts Castle" show. This
nighttime show will take guests through familiar Harry Potter scenes
with holiday music. Make sure to stay after the show to catch the

nightly snowfall in Hogsmeade! We highly recommend going to the show between 6:30-7:00 PM, as this area can get crowded.

Seasonal Melodies from the Holiday Hog Choir
During the holidays at Universal Studios Hollywood, guests have the opportunity to experience the enchanting Holiday Frog Choir as part of the festive entertainment lineup in The Wizarding World of Harry Potter. The Holiday Frog Choir, comprised of Hogwarts students adorned in their magical attire, gathers in the charming village of Hogsmeade to spread holiday cheer through the power of music. As the choir sings, the magical frogs perched atop their lily pads croak along in perfect harmony, adding whimsy and charm to the performance. The Holiday Frog Choir is a heartwarming and interactive experience that brings the wizarding world to life in a whole new way during the holidays at Universal Studios Hollywood.

MERRY GRINCHMAS IN WHO-VILLE

Grinchmas is a festive celebration that brings the whimsical world of Who-Ville to life in the heart of the park. With numerous shows, delicious treats, and Who-Ville characters at every turn, it's an event guests will not want to miss. The spirit of Christmas shines bright in this area despite the Grinch's mischievous antics!

Character Encounters

As guests step into the magical world of Who-Ville, they will be dazzled with all of the characters that inhabit the town. Characters such as The Mayor, Cindy Lou Who, Martha May, and, of course, the Grinch himself with his faithful companion Max are all available for photo opportunities.

PRO TIP

We highly recommend getting in line to meet the Grinch early in the day, as the line to meet him gets long later in the day!

Live Shows and Activities in Who-Ville

Guests can watch the beloved characters from Dr. Seuss' classic tale, "How the Grinch Stole Christmas," come to life in spectacular live performances. Be delighted by dazzling musical numbers, whimsical storytelling, and enchanting interactions that capture the true meaning of the holiday season.

One of the newest, and cutest, shows is Storytime with Cindy-Lou Who. Join Cindy-Lou Who for a live reading of "How The Grinch Stole Christmas" and then stay for a photo opportunity. This is a show children of all ages will enjoy. There is limited seating, so we recommend guests arrive about 15-20 minutes prior to the show for a spot!

Another fabulous live event is the Wholiday Tree Lighting Ceremony. During this ceremony, guests will watch The Grinch, The Mayor, Cindy-Lou Who, and other amazing characters from the classic storybook tale light the 65-foot Suessian tree! It is so beautiful!

Finally, another amazing performance that was recently introduced is the Who-Bee Doo-Wops group. This exciting new daytime performance featuring the Who-Bee Doo-Wops group is Who-Ville's latest musical sensation! This energetic ensemble rocks out to hip-swinging, bell-ringing, holiday classics, creating a festive atmosphere that has Whos and guests alike tapping their feet and singing along. With their dynamic performances and catchy tunes, the Who-Bee Doo-Wops bring an extra dose of holiday cheer to Universal Studios Hollywood, making it a season to remember for all who attend!

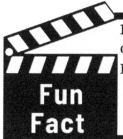

First Book is a nonprofit charity that donates books to kids in need when a postcard is sent to the Grinch! So, be sure to visit the Post Office in Who-Ville to send one and participate in this generous donation!

UNIVERSAL STUDIOS HOLLYWOOD EVE

As the sun sets, the real party begins! EVE transforms Universal Studios Hollywood into a nighttime wonderland with multiple party areas. Dance to the beats of live DJs, strike a pose at numerous photo stations, and soak in the festive atmosphere. Each party zone offers a unique vibe, so guests can find the perfect spot to dance, laugh, and celebrate with friends. Start the day with exhilarating rides, shows, and attractions then dive into an unforgettable New Year's Eve celebration! The highlight of the night is the spectacular midnight countdown. As the clock ticks closer to midnight, gather with fellow revelers to welcome the New Year. Then, get ready for a jaw-dropping fireworks display that lights up the sky with brilliant colors and dazzling effects, all set to a soundtrack of some favorite tunes.

Some of the best and most memorable times to visit Universal Studios Hollywood are during their special events. Whether looking for family fun or adult entertainment, there is an event taking place throughout the year for everyone! Do all of them sound too exciting to miss? Upgrade to an annual pass, so you can experience them all!

UNIVERSAL STUDIOS HOLLYWOOD FOR TODDLERS, TEENS, AND ADULTS

Universal Studios Hollywood has something for everyone! There is so much to see and do when visiting this destination! Attractions, entertainment, character meet-and-greets, and more away everyone, of all ages, in the park!

STROLLER RENTALS

If a guest needs a stroller rental for their day, they are available on a first-come, first-served basis. Once inside the park, rentals can be found across from the Universal Studios Store near the main entrance. Currently, a single stroller rental is $18 and double stroller rental is $25.

HEIGHT REQUIREMENTS AND CHILD SWAP

All attractions require children to be at least 48 inches tall to ride **without** a supervising companion. A supervising companion is defined as a person 14 years of age or older who meets all other ride requirements. Each attraction has specific height requirements. For the safety of the child, Universal is very strict with these requirements. Each child may be measured at a ride entrance to ensure child and ride safety.

If a child is too short, Child Swap can be used! To utilize Child Swap, there must be at least two adults in the travel party. At the entrance of an attraction, guests should tell the team member they want to "child swap." The team member will allow everyone, including young children, to enter the attraction. When the guest reaches the loading area, one adult will ride the attraction. The other adult will wait in the Child Swap location with the other children. Once the riding adult disembarks and takes over supervision of the children in the Child Swap area, the other adult can then ride! A third member of the party, either an adult or an older child, can ride twice, once with each switching-off adult, so the switching-off adult does not have to ride alone!

Each ride and attraction has Child Swap available at Universal Studios Hollywood.

RIDES AND ATTRACTIONS FOR CHILDREN

Little ones have a lot to choose from at Universal Studios Hollywood with two immersive play areas- one located in each lot. The Upper Lot play area is the Super Silly Fun Land which is a recreation of the amusement park in Despicable Me. It Includes a splash area, carnival games, and a Minions-themed Silly Swirly ride. In the Lower Lot, there is DinoPlay which offers children the ability to explore a full-size TRex skull, dinosaur eggs, and fossils!

For the kids that are a bit taller but not quite ready for the thrill rides, they can ride Life of Pets: Off the Leash (minimum height 34 inches), Kung Fu Panda, Despicable Me: Minion Mayhem (minimum height 40 inches), Flight of the Hippogriff (minimum height 39 inches), The Simpsons Ride (minimum height 40 inches), and Mario Kart: Bowser's Challenge (minimum height 40 inches).

RIDES AND ATTRACTIONS FOR TEENS AND ADULTS

For those looking for more thrill, you have many options! Inside of the Upper Lot, guests will find Harry Potter and the Forbidden Journey (minimum height 48 inches). Down inside the Lower Lot, thrill rides include Jurassic World (minimum height 42 inches), Revenge of the Mummy (minimum height 48 inches), and Transformers- The Ride 3D (minimum height 40 inches).

ATTRACTIONS FOR ALL

Never skip the Studio Tour! On this tour, guests will visit a real working studio, learning about some of the most popular movies and shows! Guests will even get to enjoy special attractions that immerse them in the movie sets, special effects use, picture cars, and movie making!

Guests also cannot miss theWaterWorld Show located in the Upper Lot! This show takes guests on a journey to find dry land, experiencing watersport exhibitions, fireworks, and world-class entertainment!

Also, be sure to be on the lookout for characters that are roaming around the park for meet-and-greets, photo opportunities, and fun interactions!

As you can see, Universal Studios Hollywood has many rides and entertainment options for all ages! With the right planning, there is something here for everyone to enjoy! Advanced planning is highly recommended, so this is the best reason to work with a Marvelous Mouse Travels' agent on your next adventure!

WHAT TO PACK

You have worked with your Marvelous Mouse Travels' agent to plan the perfect Universal Studios Hollywood vacation! So, what's next? One of the most common questions now is, "What do I need to pack!?"

Here is a helpful list of items you should pack for your upcoming adventure:

ESSENTIALS
- Breathable, Athletic Wear *(for theme parks)*
- Comfortable Walking Shoes *(you could walk upwards of five miles on theme park days, so tennis shoes/sneakers are most recommended)*
- Casual, Comfortable Wear
- Lightweight Jacket *(seasonal)*
- Hats/Visors
- Sunscreen
- Aloe *(for sunburns)*
- Fanny Pack or Small Backpack
- Portable Power Bank/Charger
- Personal Medications
- Cash for Tips *(bell services, valet, room service, etc.)*
- Important Documents *(health insurance information, government-issued ID, plane tickets)*
- Universal Studios Hollywood Travel Documents
- The Official Universal Studios Hollywood App *(downloaded on phone)*
- MOST importantly, your copy of **A Marvelous Guide to Universal Studios Hollywood!**

FOR YOUR ROOM
- Toiletries *(hanging toiletry bags are great for keeping your items organized and helps with crowded countertops)*
- Phone/Watch/Camera Chargers
- Surge Protector/Power Strip and Extension Cord *(if need to charge multiple electronics)*

- Baby Items *(pacifiers, diapers, baby wipes, baby food/formula, bottles)*
- Laundry Bags
- Laundry Detergent, Soap, and Dryer Sheets *(if utilizing on-site laundry services)*
- Stain Remover
- Sound Machine

FOR THE THEME PARKS
- Lanyards *(this is the best way to keep your tickets, hotel room key, Express Passes, ID's organized)*
- Stroller *(for smaller kids; rentals are available in the theme parks)*
- Stroller Rain Cover
- Stroller Fan *(seasonal)*
- Wheelchair *(rentals are available in the theme parks)*
- Snacks and Water/Sports Drinks *(glass containers, food requiring preparation, and outside alcoholic beverages are not allowed inside theme parks)*
- Refillable Water Bottles *(there are refilling stations available)*
- Drinking Straws *(stainless steel recommended)*
- Rain Ponchos/Umbrella
- Camera
- Hand Sanitizer
- Misting Fan/Neck Fan *(seasonal)*
- Cooling Towels *(seasonal)*
- Hydration Tablets or packets *(seasonal)*
- Motion-Sickness Medication
- Extra Entertainment such as Playing Cards, Tablets, Books, or Mobile Games *(for waiting in line)*
- Small First Aid Kit
- Headphones *(for sensory disorders)*
- Universal Merchandise purchased in advance *(wands, robes, hats, etc.)*
- Swim Shoes *(required to enter the splash zone at Super Silly Fun Land)*
- Swimsuits *(if desired for splash zone at Super Silly Fun Land)*

FOR RESORT POOLS *(if applicable)*

- Swimsuits
- Swim Shoes or Flip Flops
- Beach Bag
- Bug Spray
- Sunglasses
- Waterproof Phone Pouch
- Waterproof Cameras

ACCESSIBILITY

ATTRACTIONS ASSISTANCE PASS

If guests are visiting Universal Studios Hollywood and unable to wait for extended periods in a traditional queue, they can apply to take advantage of their Attractions Assistance Pass. In order to apply, guests must obtain an IBCCES Individual Accessibility Card (IAC) at least 48 hours prior to their visit. They can register and apply for the IAC at: www.AccessibilityCard.org. If they are approved for the IAC, a Universal Team Member will reach out to discuss their needs.

HEARING DISABILITIES

If a guest requires a sign language interpreter, they will need to make the request a week in advance by contacting Guest Relations or calling 1-800-864-8377 (option 9).

They can also obtain assistive listening devices at Guest Services for no additional charge. There is also video remote interpreting available at both First Aid and Guest Relations. Closed Captioning is available at the following attractions: Despicable Me: Minion Mayhem, Dreamworks Theatre Featuring Kung Fu Panda, The Secret Life of Pets: Off the Leash, The Simpsons Ride, and the Studio Tour.

VISION DISABILITIES

Guests with vision disabilities can obtain show scripts in both braille and large font format at Guest Services. If using a white cane and riding a ride that cannot accommodate it, a Team member can hold it for the guest while riding.

White Cane

ALLOWED IN RIDE VEHICLE	NOT ALLOWED IN RIDE VEHICLE	ALLOWED IN RIDE VEHICLE IF COLLAPSIBLE AND STORED IN POUCH
• Despicable Me Minion Mayhem • Silly Swirly Fun Ride • Transformers: The Ride 3D • The Simpsons Ride • The World-Famous Studio Tour	• Harry Potter and the Forbidden Journey	• Flight of the Hippogriff • Revenge of the Mummy - The Ride

ACCESSIBILITY ASSISTANCE FOR WHEELCHAIRS AND ECVS

Universal Studios Hollywoods strives to provide an accessible experience for all guests! They have made all of their ride queues, restaurants, and shopping facilities wheelchair accessible. There are also accessible viewing sections for stage shows.

If guests need wheelchair or ECV assistance, both are available on a first-come, first-served basis. Once inside the park, rentals can be found across from the Universal Studios Store near the main entrance. Currently, wheelchair rentals cost $20 and ECV rentals cost $60.

There is also a shuttle that can take guests between the Upper and Lower Lots. Guests in ECVs or other Power-Driven Mobility Devices must transfer to shuttle seating.

Mobility Accesibility

GUESTS MUST BE ABLE TO TRANSFER TO THE RIDE VEHICLE (YOU MUST HAVE SOMEONE IN YOUR PARTY ASSIST, TEAM MEMBERS MAY NOT ASSIST)	GUESTS ARE ABLE TO REMAIN IN OR TRANSFER TO A MANUAL WHEELCHAIR (PROVIDED AT RIDE)	GUESTS MAY REMAIN IN THEIR ECV OR MOTORIZED WHEELCHAIR
• Flight of the Hippogriff • Harry Potter and the Forbidden Journey • Jurassic World- The Ride • Revenge of the Mummy - The Ride • Silly Swirly Fun Ride • The Simpsons Ride • Transformers: The Ride 3D • Mario Kart: Bowser's Challenge	• Studio Tour • Secret Life of Pets: Off the Leash	• Despicable Me Minion Mayhem • Dino Play for Kids • Dreamworks Theatre Featuring Kung Fu Panda

PROSTHETIC LIMBS

Certain rides and attractions require guests to either secure or remove their prosthetics prior to riding. For full details, please refer to the Guide for Rider Safety and Accessibility.

SERVICE ANIMALS

Service animals are welcome in all shows, shopping locations, and restaurants. There are also service animal relief areas in the following locations: Upper Lot next to the entrance to the Studio Tour, Lower Lot across from the Jurassic World Lagoon, and outside of the park near the accessible parking, adjacent to the security checkpoint. While many rides can accommodate service animals, some do not. The rides that cannot accommodate service animals do have kennels for use while riding.

Service Animals

Universal Studios Hollywood
Accesibility

ATTRACTION/RIDE VEHICLE CAN ACCOMODATE SERVICE ANIMALS	ATTRACTION/RIDE VEHICLE NOT ACCESSIBLE FOR SERVICE ANIMALS. SERVICE ANIMAL KENNEL AVAILABLE ON REQUEST
• Despicable Me Minion Mayhem • Dino Play for Kids • Dreamworks Theatre Featuring Kung Fu Panda • Silly Swirly Fun Ride • The Simpsons Ride • Studio Tour • Super Silly Fun Land • Transformers: The Ride 3D • WaterWorld	• Flight of the Hippogriff • Harry Potter and the Forbidden Journey • Jurassic World - The Ride • Mario Kart: Bowser's Challenge • Revenge of the Mummy - The Ride • The Secret Life of Pets: Off the Leash

OXYGEN TANKS

Guests with oxygen tanks (compressed and liquid) cannot bring them on many rides due to the intense movement of ride vehicles and special effects. Tanks are only permitted on the following attractions: Dreamworks Theatre Featuring Kung Fu Panda (stationary seating only) and WaterWorld.

FIRST AID AND FAMILY CENTER

There are two first aid stations- one in the Upper Lot and one in the Lower Lot. The Upper Lot first aid station is located next to French Street Bistro, and the Lower Lot first aid station is next to the Studio Store. There are nurses on duty to assist guests, as needed.

The Family Center is located outside the entrance to WaterWorld. It has the following amenities: two private nursing/quiet rooms, sink, microwave, accessible bathrooms with changing tables, and a vending machine with necessities such as bandaids, chapstick, benadryl, and other items. Additionally, Universal Studios Hollywood recently added a quiet room in the Family Center that can be used for up to 30 minutes; this is a great spot for guests that have sensory disorders.

ACCESSIBLE AND FAMILY RESTROOMS

Each bathroom has at least one accessible stall. If guests require a private, single-stall, family bathroom, they are located at the following locations: CityWalk (next to Sunsations), Upper Lot outside the Animation Studio Store, Super Silly Fun Land, and near Jurassic World.

ACCESSIBILITY AT HOTELS

We highly recommend staying at either the Sheraton Universal Hotel or Hilton Los Angeles/Universal City if guests have any accessibility needs. Both hotels offer multiple types of accessible rooms and accessible transportation or walking paths to the park. Because they are located so close, they are also convenient if breaks are needed throughout the day.

For more details on specific ride accommodations, please refer to the "Guide for Rider Safety and Accessibility."

FREQUENTLY ASKED QUESTIONS

HOW MANY DAYS DO YOU NEED TO VISIT THE PARK?

We recommend one day with a VIP Tour or Express Passes; without a VIP Tour or Express Passes, we recommend two days.

WHERE DO I PARK IF I'M GOING FOR ONE DAY?

Universal Studios Hollywood offers general parking, preferred parking, and valet parking.

HOW CLOSE IS UNIVERSAL STUDIOS HOLLYWOOD TO DISNEYLAND?

Universal Studios Hollywood is 35 miles from Disneyland. You can expect the drive to be approximately 1.5 hours due to traffic conditions.

COULD I STAY AT DISNEYLAND AND VISIT FOR ONE DAY?

You can definitely visit for one day with Express Passes or a VIP Tour!

WHAT RIDES STAY OPEN IN BAD WEATHER?

All indoor rides will stay open in the event of inclement weather. Depending on the severity of the weather, the outdoor rides will close. Luckily, southern California does not have many days with bad weather!

WHAT IS THE BEST TIME TO VISIT?

The best time to visit is late August and early September.

ARE THERE ACCOMMODATIONS FOR GUESTS WITH DISABILITIES?

For guests who require an attraction queue accommodation, an IBCCES Individual Accessibility Card (IAC) must be obtained. Register at **AccessibilityCard.org** at least 48 hours prior to visiting the park. For guests using a mobility device, an IAC is not needed, as all attraction queues are accessible.

WHAT ARE THE BEST NEARBY HOTELS TO STAY?

The best places to stay are The Garland, Hilton Los Angeles/Universal City, and Sheraton Universal Hotel. These are all nearby hotels and each have their own section with additional information in this Guide.

DO INTERACTIVE WANDS WORK ON BOTH COASTS?

Yes! Your interactive wand will work at both Universal Studios Hollywood and Universal Orlando Resort!

WHAT DO I PACK?

For a day at the park, you should always bring either a backpack or fanny pack to hold a photo ID, credit cards, cash, and a portable battery pack for your phone. If you are not staying at a nearby hotel, you should also bring any necessary medication you would need throughout the day. If you are visiting during the summer, you should consider bringing a refillable cup to stay hydrated and a cooling fan or towels!

WHERE DO I START IN THE PARK?

We recommend starting in the Lower Lot (with a Super Nintendo World Early Access ticket) then moving into the Upper Lot for the remainder of your visit!

Made in the USA
Coppell, TX
10 December 2024

42001206R00075